# HOW TO WIN AT FAILURE

## Welcome to Disappointment, just don't stay too long

D1522234

## by Denice Volk Reich

# Note from the Author

This book is meant to help others navigate life, no matter what path they choose. Only you can figure out how to live a successful, happy life, despite the circumstances.

The puzzle is the journey of life that teaches you about the pieces that fit and do not fit.

Deal with things as they are and make the best of it. This is your life, and the actions (good and bad) of others should not define you. When you're in despair, seek out groups that will empower you to succeed. Be skeptical of professionals.

Live your life forward, understand it backwards. Do not let the past control the outcome of your future.

This is a book about how to be successful, no matter how life flattens you. It is about persistence and the right attitude.

As I have always said, "If it is meant to be, it is up to me."

# About the Author

Denice Reich is a well-known pioneer in the Denver real estate market. She was considered at one time to be one of the 500 most powerful women in real estate. She is a part of the RE/MAX Circle of Legends, Hall of Fame Chairman's Club, and has received their Lifetime Achievement Award. She is an advocate for children, and was a member of the governor of Colorado's task force on childcare. She started the organization PAACC (Public Awareness About Abuse in Childcare), and has appeared on nationally syndicated shows to further childcare safety regulations, including:

Oprah Winfrey
Larry King
48 Hours
and
The Today Show

HOW TO WIN AT FAILURE
Welcome To Disappointment, just don't stay too long.
Copyright © 2022 Denice C. Reich, Inc.
All rights reserved.

Cover Design and Editor: Justin Petersen
Author's website – dreichauthor.com
True Story| Inspirational | Success | Empowerment

# Acknowledgement

*To Miss America, Marilyn VanDebur Atler, for her courage in exposing the lifelong effects of sexual abuse inflicted on children.*

# Table of Contents

# Aspen, the Source of my Independence

## Broken Spirit to Perfection

I want to tell the story of what I have overcome, in the hope it may become part of someone else's survival guide. My story begins with Aspen. Aspen has been the main part of my life. The history of Aspen in the late 1940s and the 1950s was a time in America when I grew up with hardworking, independent characters. They were a part of mountain towns in Colorado. The difficult times were mixed with common sense, humor, and community.

As a child I was raised amongst miners, shop owners, and ranchers. The town had a population of 250, and all those residents were accepted as equals.

The beauty of the mountains surrounded the town. As children, we were free to explore mines, abandoned houses, and lakes and rivers. This is where I watched the persistence of the residents, and learned the gratitude to like what I had, not want what I did not have. They lived as Churchill famously said, "Success is going from failure to failure with enthusiasm." **No matter what the hardships were, whether a flooded mine, or an avalanche that took down the mill, the residents and business owners of Aspen were a determined lot.**

I was born in Denver, Colorado, the youngest of four children. In most ways we were a typical 1940s-era family: hardworking father, stay-at-home mother, energetic children. We looked like a happy, ordinary family, but we had our secrets, as most families do.

My father—my hero—grew up in Ohio. At the age of sixteen, at the urging of his parents, he attended college at the Colorado School of Mines. Russell "Rut" Volk was an extraordinary athlete. He was driven to excel and was the star center on the School of Mines football team. In four years, he never lost a dual-meet match in wrestling or boxing. He was the regional boxing champion who somehow found time to play basketball and baseball, earning fifteen letters during his time at the School of Mines, a school record that stands to this day.

My father was so revered that the school inducted him into the Hall of Fame and named its gymnasium in his honor. After graduation, he took a teaching job at the college and studied for his master's degree in Petroleum Engineering. It was during that time that he started his career, forming the Plains Exploration Company with other faculty members. The company drilled wildcat wells in eastern Colorado and Kansas. He taught me never to give up, no matter what happened.

It was during his senior year that he met my mother. At eighteen, she had moved from Denver to New York City to be a professional ballet dancer, which was a scandalous decision in those days. Most women were married by eighteen and starting families. Women who went to work, especially in the entertainment industry, were considered brash and unconventional. It was not a good time to be brash or unconventional in America. New York City might as well have been the moon, but my mom defied the odds and ignored the gossip.

She loved to dance and perform, never loving anything else as much. The legendary producer John Golden sent a handwritten letter to my grandmother assuring her that "Alice is behaving very properly." He explained that she was not doing any of the things some women do, such as dating stagehands or running wild in the city.

My mother had some early successes—appearing in stage shows and getting small roles in silent movies—but she wasn't a star. At some point, the societal pressures and expectations of what a woman should be led her to return to Denver, and settle down.

My father had spotted a newspaper article featuring a photo of the hometown dancer/actress who was scheduled for a rare performance at a theater in downtown Denver. Pop was so taken by her pretty face that he clipped her photo from the paper and pinned it inside his locker at the School of Mines. He was surprised when my uncle stopped by and asked why Rut had a photo of his sister pinned in his locker. He was smitten, and began courting my mother in earnest.

It took a few years before Alice agreed to marry Rut, and it was big news in Denver when they tied the knot. She was twenty-four, and

## Actress and Former Grid Star to Wed

My parents—Russell "Rut" Volk and Alice Volk.

everyone was relieved she had settled down. She gave up her career and settled into a life as a fulltime housewife.

Soon, she had two boys and two girls. She was never fulfilled with her life as a housewife and mother, it had become a disappointment. The endless cooking, cleaning and changing diapers filled her everyday life. Maybe she just did not really want to be a mother. Whatever it was, she was very unhappy, and she took this unhappiness out on her four kids. We bore the brunt of her anger and sadness because at that time women had no other avenue to express their feelings.

She did have an adventurous spirit, in 1945, she took an extraordinary risk by insisting the family move to Aspen. She had looked it up on a map, and there was only one road in, which she argued would protect the children during the polio epidemic that was sweeping through Colorado. Radio news reports encouraged parents to keep their children inside. Mom had no interest in being cooped up all day with four children in the city, while my pop was away with his busy career, scouting potential oil fields. In later years he was one of the engineers who discovered the Eastern Julesburg Basin, and always said that he never received a penny for the discovery because he had to pay all the investors. He always said, **"They could always take the money, but they could never take his joy of discovery."** My mother's efforts worked, and she did not have to stay inside with four kids every day and was able to achieve one of her personal dreams, living in the mountains.

During the week, she walked down to the Roaring Fork River that flowed through the east end of Aspen. She saw a shack with an old miner and asked, "Do you know of any property for sale?" He did, and he sold his own 400-square foot, two-room shack and all the land surrounding it to my parents for $17.57.

Denice and her siblings in front of property purchased for $17.57

Our new home had no interior plumbing, no heat, and no running water. We used an outhouse, we did not like to use this outhouse, and would ask Margie McCadden if we could use hers since it was on the river, and we could watch our waste go down the river. Mom sent us with a bar of soap to bathe in the river, which was breathtakingly cold, even in the middle of summer—but I loved it! In later years, we got a kerosene tank for heat in the shack, which was a big deal in those days. Otherwise, our home remained as rustic as rustic could be.

When purchased, it was filled with old newspapers, rotting food, and empty liquor bottles. With each new meal, the original miner had just covered his mess with a fresh newspaper. Even outside, every bush was covered with empty liquor bottles.

Cleaning this before moving in was a huge job. From all reports, my mom took on this task, happily making it her own home.

Aspen in the 1940s was filled with hardy, colorful characters: Grandma Sandstrom (one of the older women in town) made us Swedish cardamom rolls, still sweet in my memory. She sold goat milk to the town and raised goats where the river split below the trestle, an area now known

Privy over river - 1940s

Denice, Grandma Sanstrom

as Newberry Park, but used to be known as "Goat Island." Her sons lived in a shack up the street from us, and they were almost "pickled" from alcohol. One of her sons was a singer known as "Hoofy." He sang "My Wild Irish Rose" and "The Yellow Rose of Texas" from the top of a tall ladder. They were the only survivors in a family that had lost four other men in the mines, including Grandma's husband. The men were all alcoholics and had been killed stumbling drunk into mining equipment or falling down mine shafts. Grandma Sandstrom was typical of a western woman of the time, surviving without her husband by baking rolls and selling them along with goat milk to the town. I was very influenced growing up by her kindness, and her determined spirit.

5

When our shack needed shoring up because the timbers underneath were rotting, my dad hired two miners, Pope Rowland and Lynus Lynch, who crawled underneath on their hands and knees and lifted the house while he shoved under new support logs. He paid them each a bottle of whiskey, and they were as happy as they could be. Alcohol was often a better form of payment than cash back then.

Our home was in a neighborhood known originally as Swedish Hollow, later as Oklahoma Flats, and always known as "the wrong side of town." In the early mining years, about 24 Swedish families, each with their own 400-square-foot, or smaller shack, worked the Smuggler Mine above us. When they moved, they abandoned these homes, and those shacks sat vacant. When the price of silver crashed, only three of the original Swedish families remained in the area.

We were in the poorest section of town, but thought it was a wonderland. The Roaring Fork River surrounded the neighborhood.

Every Tuesday, the old steam engine train came in just below the Jerome Hotel. My fondest memory is of the engineer blowing the whistle. The kids in town ran to ride the train across the trestle to the Smuggler Mine, which today is the oldest silver mine in the United States. We played on the old steam shovel and on the mine dumps and we slid down the mine pilings until we were covered in black dust. We were in kid heaven.

The trestle above Oklahoma Flats.

We explored the abundance of abandoned sheds and commercial buildings in town. The walls still stood but the roofs had caved in from snow loads. Most of the houses had been abandoned, with doors left open and furniture and personal items left untouched. Many other buildings in town had been burned from fires, even the opera house and old drug store. It was a playground for us. The only time we were careful was of the old cesspools and wells, so we would not fall in. Our knowledge to be careful was not learned from a parent, but from a neighbor boy falling in, and emerging covered in human waste.

The Koch lumber buildings were amazing because they still had bins of handles, wagon wheels, sleighs, brass beds and ladders, just as they were abandoned. Dorothy Shaw owned the lumber yard and a lot of abandoned properties. We would wait until she had checked the yard in the middle of each day, then we snuck inside to play. She became, in our imaginative young minds, an evil witch who might be lurking behind some prop, and that made the exploration more thrilling.

During haying season, we went to the Marolt barn, drove the tractor and old jeep. The parents loved when we came over, and let us just be kids.

When we wanted a swimming pool, we dug a giant hole, then figured out how to redirect the ditch water that ran through Oklahoma flats to connect to our freshly dug mud hole. We soaked until our skin shriveled up, and our teeth chattered. Because it was just a mudhole, we took my mom's detergent to try and make it cleaner. She was not happy.

We learned to fish with dynamite or M-80s. We would climb on top of a large boulder and tie the explosive to a long stick, light, and quickly place it in the river. We would then scoop up the stunned fish. When mom was in a good mood, she fried them up with cornmeal for a special treat. To this day, I marvel at any- one who has the patience to hold a fishing pole.

We made a lot of friends—Tim and Jeannie Willoughby, the Marolts, Sandra Beck and Sheri Gerbaz, to name a few. Bill Herron, an old miner from the Smuggler, kept a house full of tools and small porcelain dishes used for assaying metals. He was always happy to see the neighborhood kids and he never scolded us if we got into things. We would have tea parties using his assay dishes. Pop let us have the tea parties, but forbade us to ride in Bill's car, as the dynamite Bill kept in the back was crystallized and Pop was afraid it might explode at any time.

We got to know some of our neighbors, like "Midnight Mary" and "Slops," ladies of the evening who provided their services to the men who had worked the mines. They lived in the trailer at the curve on Spring Street in Oklahoma Flats. Their trailer often rocked. Sometimes, they got into huge fights. Mom always told us, "Stay away from those women, they carry diseases."

My sister and I learned a lot from some of the mothers, especially Albina Gerbaz and Alice Vaugner, who taught us how to sew as a part of the 4-H program and we put on fashion shows at the Isis Theater. We felt like New York models, though the clothes were ugly and poorly made. When the fashion shows were done, we took our clothing to the thrift store. Woe to the shopper who purchased one of our outfits!

At *The Prince* Albert Hotel, we dropped mattresses out the windows, so we could bring them home for when we had company. It's just the way things were. Everyone borrowed from each other and returned borrowed items in better condition than they found them. It was an unwritten rule.

Pope Rowland, a fine brewer of dandelion wine, was so industrious that we never saw a dandelion growing in Aspen. Pope harvested them before they had a chance to spread. Today, the parks and lawns are covered in dandelions, and I think it's a shame that the environmentally correct people in town haven't figured out how to harvest them. Pope was no snob. He'd ferry his latest concoction across the footbridge to the good citizens who lived in the nicer sections of town. Everyone loved his dandelion wine. My dad always said it would kill you or make you blind. It was a mainstay of the town during the summers.

There was plenty of dandelion wine, but no detox centers. When a man got too dependent on alcohol, his friends attached him to a tree near the river with a long chain to sweat out the delirium tremens. They left him with basic survival equipment, and a fishing pole and gun. The prevailing wisdom was that in a few months, he would be "good and cured" or "good and dead."

The singer Hoofy was enjoying a bit of that fine concoction when he announced to my eldest brother that he'd planted an "A-bomb" (1 stick of dynamite) to take down a particularly bad anthill in front of his house. My brother assumed it was the wine talking and settled in at our home for our regular game of Monopoly, to which I attribute my future success in real estate because I learned the importance of location and good property.

Suddenly, a loud boom shook the house, shattered the windows, and sent the Monopoly pieces flying. The sheriff arrested Hoofy, and my pop and other men in town placed bets on when he would be released. The question

Aspen neighbors

wasn't about the length of his sentence, but how long the sheriff's wife would put up with cooking for him. My pop won the bet! That was a huge deal because we were able to purchase plywood to cover the entire inside of the home, making it airtight (and ugly beyond belief).

My brothers thought the whole thing was a hoot, and started planting their own explosives around town. They put an M-80 in the privy when my sister and I were inside it, and the explosion caused a stinking mess. Mom made the boys sleep outside that entire summer as punishment.

My neighborhood friends, siblings, and I made our own fun in Aspen. We felt like everything belonged to us, and each day brought a new adventure. For many wonderful years, the whole town was our playground. We hiked, camped, and played. We explored all of Hunter Creek and floated in the Salvation Ditch (known as The Sally) on inner tubes. We played in the flumes and swam in the massive barrel that contained the Aspen Water Supply. Often dead birds, chipmunks, skunks, and raccoons floated in the water tank, but they didn't deter us. We just swam on the other side.

Being allowed to roam freely in Aspen taught us to be self-reliant and fearless, not like the silver spoon Aspen kids of today, and their helicopter parents. My siblings and I were always devising ways to earn money. We had an old tent we would take uptown to the vacant property (now the Paradise Bakery) and set up a lemonade stand for the tourists. We once got into big trouble for stealing glass pop bottles out of the back of Elder's Market and reselling them to the market for two cents apiece. We got into even bigger trouble selling off Mom's antiques. When my mom went to Glenwood Springs, we'd sneak some of her antiques and sell them to tourists for ten cents each. It was not a good idea.

Our first "real" job came from Johnny Herron, who hired us to wash his car. We were so proud and so pleased, especially having heard the stories of how Mr. Herron had courted Frances Willoughby for decades, unable to marry her because Irish and English didn't mix in those days. When his mother finally passed, he married Frances. My sister and I thought it was so romantic.

My brothers worked at the Stein Ranch and, like the rest of the town's residents, walked along the train tracks, now the Rio Grande Trail, to work. They later worked at the cinder block factory in Oklahoma Flats, that Tex Bones started.

Once, Pop took us uptown to see the "Eighth Wonder of the World"—a concrete mixer truck. It was nearly impossible to get a vehicle like that up the mountain road, so everyone was curious about it. "You're going to see the best part of America," Pop said, and explained how fine it was that they had invented a truck that mixed its own cement. He spoke of the great ingenuity of America. He installed a sense of "awe" for

America, we were all so proud. To this day, I still get a thrill whenever I see a concrete mixer truck, and I must stop and remind myself it's not that big of a deal now.

It ended up backing into an old cesspool in town, and that was the end of the concrete business in Aspen for several years. Cesspools were more prevalent in Aspen then even the present generation of men who wear spandex bicycle shorts. In my opinion, real men don't wear tights.

On Sundays, our family often picnicked with townspeople near the headwaters of Maroon Creek. Mom would cook lots of chicken in a Dutch oven and Pop would carry it to a rock just above the inlet. It was our spot. Those picnics were our weekly entertainment. Everyone would bring food to share.

Our parents often got together and went to the T-Lazy 7 Ranch to take bets on which horse would die next. Many of the horses were starving to death because the owners couldn't afford to feed them. They died with their legs sticking up in the air. There was no television, so the town created its own entertainment.

Another source of interest was when the sheep herds wandered down from Hunter Creek and came right through the city, stirring up a ton of dust in an unplanned parade.

Beck & Bishop's was the local grocery store, the place for gossip, and Aspen's unofficial "telephone." Women did their daily shopping there and spent an hour or more chatting and having coffee at the back of the store. We didn't have telephones, so gossip was the best way for my mom to find out what was happening in town. Savaha and Lawrence Elisha owned the Hotel Jerome – they were amongst the hardest working people in town. The town was built with an unconditional bond of helping each other.

Back then, Aspen was a true community. Everyone trusted and helped one another. If someone needed something, a neighbor provided it. If someone hit hard times, someone helped. People were more valuable than property or material wealth. The town dump helped many residents furnish their homes as Aspen became more affluent.

In 1948, when everyone in Aspen was losing their property because they couldn't pay their taxes, two miners approached my mom wanting to sign over the deed to an empty lot in the center of town because they owed $125 in back taxes. Mom gave them two bottles of whiskey and pop paid the back taxes. That lot is now The Paradise Bakery. Back then, Judge Shaw's wife, Dorothy, would get firsthand information on tax titles and purchase many of the properties for pennies on the dollar these miners didn't want Dorothy to get their property, which is why they approached my mom. Pop hated that we had to pay taxes on that vacant lot. In 1956, he leased the land to an oil company at $350 per month, who used it for a gas station until 1986. He was so pleased with the deal. He came home that day and told us we were the wealthiest family in Aspen, and we probably were. It gives a perspective of how poor the town used to be.

Our father would engage us on trips to Denver or Aspen with educational facts. He would delight in repeating Kipling's poetry or making us name all the famous conductors or classical music composers.

He told us, "Someday, kiddies, there will be a tunnel under the mountain to the other side and we'll not have to go over Loveland Pass when it is so dangerous." He told us the town of Dillon would be under a big lake. We would no longer be able to fill the car and drain the family at the only gas station on the route. If you did not relieve yourself in Dillon, you would have to hold it until Aspen. We passed the town of Kokomo on our way to Leadville. He said, "Look carefully. Kokomo will be gone in 20 years as the mountain at Climax mine will cover the entire town and valley with mine tailings." He would explain how incredible everything was that was happening in America because everyone worked hard and was so tough.

He always reminded us of his Colorado School of Mines friend, Frank Cobalt, who ran the Climax Mine and how that saved America in the war. The ore produced was used to strengthen steel.

**He was very proud of America and constantly taught us how lucky we were to live in such a great country.**

When we got to Independence Pass, there was a lot of swearing if someone was coming up the road. It was always scary because we would have to back up to let them pass. There was only room for one car. It often had a very steep drop. He would say, "Son of a Bitch" when he met another car. When they got past each other, everyone was relieved. We always called it Son-of-a-Bitch Pass instead of Independence Pass.

One of the best things about Aspen was that my mom was marginally happier there than she ever was in Denver. I was happier there, too. I loved the entire town and all the people in it. Every moment spent there was precious to me. I always felt at home there because Aspen was a place for the fiercely independent—and that was me.

Although my mother was noticeably happier in Aspen, she never talked of her own childhood. That was the norm for that generation. The saying was, "Never hang the family laundry out." The family secret tragedies were laughed about inside the family. For example, her Aunt Lockhardt killed herself by walking into the ocean and drowning. She was only 19 years old, and it was never questioned or talked about. My mother had a difficult childhood, of that, I am sure. Perhaps that is why I have empathy for her horrific treatment of my spirit at a young age.

Her own sister, Beverly, was kicked in the stomach while pregnant by her husband and gave birth to a boy, Bucky, who died from injuries caused by this less than a year after birth. She later married a kind man, but sadly died in childbirth, leaving 3 children.

I once saw my uncle, her brother, tie his little boy to a chair and kick his tiny legs until they bled.

Then there was my mother.... she ended up having four children of her own. She went from the theater (center stage) to a life of little more than taking care of four children with no help and no acknowledgement.

She was NOT joyful of having a family. She managed her anger by taking it out on her children. She would punish me by holding me down and giving me enemas to "Wash the bad out of me." **This taught me that I was a very bad little girl who did not belong in this world.** I didn't understand why she was so angry at me. Another thing she would do was buckle my overalls on me, so I could not remove them. Then she would tell me to, "Hold it in." When I was unable to, and would have an accident, she would get a switch, and hit me with it. She never even discussed that you start menstruating around 12 years old. When it happened to me, I stopped drinking cherry Kool-Aid. I figured that was the problem. My mother also never talked to us about sex, leaving me clueless and naïve.

**These punishments and silences served to make me even more defiant. I figured the only way to fit in the world was to be perfect, and never vulnerable.** I coped with the feelings of being alone and shamed by going elsewhere in my mind. I learned in later years this is called, disassociation. I organized my life around the fear of anyone finding out how "bad" I was. Shame was the emotion I felt throughout my childhood. I felt I was flawed, and not "good enough" to fit in the world.

Those crushing childhood wounds would lead me down a dark path of suicidal thoughts and escapes that I never quite understood.

I learned mothers can abuse their children and that stunned me. It seemed normal and I never realized that it was abuse. My mother did the same to my other siblings. She never realized the damage she inflicted on my spirit at such a young age. Years later I questioned my siblings, and my oldest brother denied it ever happened, the middle brother stated he would rather have had that than castor oil, my sister said that was just mothers' "nuttiness." Obviously, they thought it was no big deal ---yet their lives spoke differently with the levels of their own dysfunction.

My dysfunction was that I became a complete people pleaser. I had no place in the world that I wanted to fit in, so I made my world what everyone else wanted. I went forward with my idea of being perfect, never allowing events that would make me vulnerable.

Somehow that vulnerability I tried so hard to hide allowed my brothers to use their power over my sister and myself. They were 7 and 10 years older, and I looked up to them for the acceptance and affection that I craved. Instead of helping us, they hurt us badly. I would do anything they asked, even driving a stick-shift truck up Independence Pass, even though I was unable to reach the pedals. It was an example of how they used terror to exert their power over me. Many times, they threw us off a bridge into the rushing waters of the Roaring Fork River. When I was five, they held my fingers down until I said "Uncle." They tickled me until I begged for mercy.

I would especially do anything for my eldest brother because he would give me compliments. He explored my indefensible small body in ways that were unspeakable. I knew what I allowed him to do was wrong, and shameful. I coped with these feelings by going elsewhere in my mind.

**From that point on, I organized my life around the intense shame and replaced those feelings with my need for perfection.** This is how I fit in and survived. I wove the fabric of that defeating shame into a life of success. I had an insatiable need to be completely successful at everything I tried. I became the perfect cheerleader, Sweetheart Queen, runner, skier, Pan Am stewardess, and top realtor. **I fit in this world because the acknowledgements that I received for my successes gave me a feeling of belonging.** If I was not constantly improving myself, I would feel worthless. This is how I learned to survive and win.

For 40 years, I repressed these memories and focused only on my need of achieving perfection. It was only when I met Marilyn VanDerbur, a fellow incest survivor, that I became aware of connecting my behavior to my actions. **This knowledge helped me to understand the crippling wounds of sexual abuse and helped me change my behavior.**

Despite my brothers' cruelty, and their taking advantage of me, I adored them. I kept their disgusting, sadistic secrets, even when they made fun of me. Their betrayals were so deftly woven into my life choices, I dealt with them in my future life choices. I found myself choosing similarly damaging relationships to try and fix the past.

I got through the school years by dreaming of my summers in Aspen, where I was free to roam and run outdoors. Running was something I could do better than anyone else. I received praise from others, so I pushed myself to overachieve.

Overachieving became a big part of my life. My father said, "You never let yourself rest until your better is better than all the rest." I never rested at all. My father wanted me to be an Olympian and I trained as if his dream were my own. At least when I was running, I was never behind.

During my summers in Aspen, I could work. One summer, some friends and I worked at the Aspen Meadows Hotel. One guest, Mr. Adler, wasn't friendly. He was downright grumpy. So, my friends and I painted his toilet seat with honey, and short- sheeted his bed. Not a smart thing to do. We all got fired.

Most of the time, though, I was a conscientious worker. It wasn't about the money, though it was liberating to have my own money. No, the work was its own reward. I liked the satisfaction of doing a good job. I also liked the praise from my employers.

Praise gave me a sense of belonging.

A few summers, I worked part time in the Kalamaths' dry goods store in Aspen, stocking shelves and waiting on people. I helped customers fill their orders. Even as a child and as a young teen, I was displaying all the skills necessary for a successful career.

I would have loved to live in Aspen year-round, but my siblings and I couldn't attend school there. So, our mother, who had a knack for finding great property, moved our family to Cherry Hills in Denver. She bought two-and-a-half acres because she loved the view. The schools were new and had innovative education. It was a world away from Aspen and I was scared to go to junior high.

Then just inside the front door, I met Linda Freeman who became my lifelong friend. We never stopped laughing and talking. Linda was the funniest person and I gladly served as her audience. We later supported each other through marriage, divorce, children, loss of her child, and the death of our parents. We shared our life's disappointments as well as many moments of sheer joy. I am still so grateful for Linda's spirit, her laughter and her wisdom.

I devoted time to cheerleading with Linda as well as running track.

She and I were chosen as homecoming and sweetheart queens, and the other students looked up to us. We were quite a fun team.

Young girls in the 1950s were taught to dream of marriage and family. We weren't taught to dream of a career, even though women had worked for the war effort in World War II, while men were fighting overseas. So, we assumed we would get married, have babies, and live happily ever after. Like typical teenage girls, we giggled and talked about the boys in class. The truth was, though, I was never comfortable around boys. I didn't date or flirt. Instead, I threw myself into running track, skiing, cheerleading, and whatever work I could find each summer.

In high school, I didn't admit weakness or ask for help. I felt everyone was judging me, so I developed a tough outer shell, driven and determined to please everyone. Each morning I put on a mask.

I was a Volk. In the Volk family, we had a mantra: A Volk can never be sick, tired, hungry, cold, lonely, or afraid. We were expected to be strong and proud, robust and healthy, well-adjusted and independent. I worked hard to keep up the image of the flawless daughter, the perfect sister, the world-class athlete.

**It wasn't enough to be a great athlete or to keep out of trouble. I sought awards and praise because accolades would prove I was a good**

**person, and it gave me a sense of belonging.** I knew what I was supposed to be, so I faked it. My mother might have had a brief career as an actress, but I was the true actress in the family. No one put on a show better than I did, and I kept it up for years.

In 1959, my world began to change. One by one, my siblings left the house—my brothers to college, then marriage. My sister would soon graduate, too. My father's work kept him away from home most days, so I was alone a lot. When I wasn't alone,

I was with my mother.

I was sixteen, and well past the age of playing with dolls.

Yet, I still wanted to be perfect, like every other little girl.

After World War II when the men came home, no one expected women to continue working. We should no longer aspire to be like Rosie the Riveter, the temporary breadwinner.

On the surface, the 1950s was a period of peace and prosperity, the embodiment of the American Dream. Magazines showed women wearing aprons, baking cookies, smiling blandly from suburban homes, finding fulfillment in serving husbands and children, and wearing pearls and high heels as they managed their lives.

Underneath these placid suburban fantasies, however, the world was changing. In the early '50s, people worried about the "Red Scare" and communism as the Cold War was heating up. In the mid 1950s, the Civil Rights movement was gaining momentum elsewhere in the country, and the Vietnam War was already deadly for American soldiers.

But those threats and worries were not to be my concern. As a young woman, my concern was singular and simple: settle into a lifetime of domestic bliss with a husband and children.

When I thought of such a life, however, it didn't feel like bliss.

It felt like settling, and losing my independence.

I was too young to be among the first waves of women in the work-force. Yet deep down, I yearned for more, though I had no words to express what I was feeling.

I was not alone. Women everywhere were not content with housekeeping and caring for children. They'd had a taste of what it meant to work.

Some women got through the days of housewifery, tedium and monotony by popping pills or drinking. They sought therapy and were often diagnosed as unstable—by men who believed their job was to keep women even-tempered and content in their prescribed roles.

I do have to thank my mother: I grew up with a front-row seat to the hard consequences of broken dreams. I saw in her what happens when a woman quits a fulfilling career to raise a family and keep house. She had lived in New York City and worked in the glamorous entertainment industry. Giving up her career must have been terrible for her. How else could I explain her behavior? I wondered if she would have been happier if she had kept working. Perhaps she would have been nicer if she had never had children. Perhaps she would have been less bitter if she had never married at all.

All I really know is she was miserable with her life and she took that misery out on us.

So, I was miserable, too, but I couldn't show it. At sixteen, looking toward high school graduation, my choices seemed narrow as I realized that, after school, I was facing a lifetime of more of the same. There was no other choice.

I was fortunate that my father believed in education. He would send me to college. But once college ended, there would be only one path forward: domesticity.

I could not picture myself there. **I began to look for a way out. I felt a dark emptiness taking over my thoughts. I feared living more than dying. I was incredibly calm, I just no longer had the courage to live.**

I sped down the highway, looking for something to help me accomplish my task. I hit a bridge abutment head on at 80 miles an hour. The VW bug I was driving crumpled. If the motor had been in the front, it would have sliced right through me. My legs were mangled, my face was sliced open by the glass. I had broken bones, twisted joints, sprains, bruises, and cuts and abrasions. I suffered my first seizure from an injury to my brain. My Olympic running dreams vanished. After recovering from my accident, I turned my focus to getting out of the house.

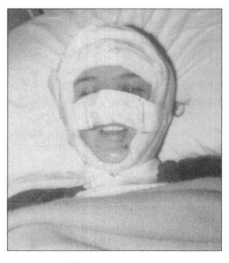

Injuries from 1960

In my high school classes, I now had to work harder than ever. In a way, it was a blessing. No one expected me to do much.

Thankfully, some of my former ability to handle complex problems came back to me, but I never fully recovered. Other students flew through homework and essays, while I labored over every word.

It was like working without a light.

Only by narrowing my focus and forcing myself to think of nothing else could I get my schoolwork done. But I did.

I thought college would give me the freedom I craved. At Colorado State University I joined a sorority and tried to make friends, but it was difficult. The other girls dated and went to parties. They stayed up late, gossiping and flipping through fashion magazines. I couldn't do any of that. It took every ounce of focus I could muster just to keep up with my classes.

Not only was my complex reasoning compromised by the head injury, but also my memory. I often forgot things as soon as I heard them. I had no ability to read something, then talk about it with any sense of understanding. I just couldn't remember what I had read.

The only way I could manage was to read every passage again and again until I had memorized every word.

It took hours of intense concentration to study for a test, and I could only hold on to so many facts at a time. So, I memorized what I needed to know for one test and kept that information in my brain by not thinking of anything else until the test was over. Hoping that I had gotten through it, I promptly forgot everything— and started over on another subject.

It was a terrible way to study and left me no time for anything else. Other students went out and had fun. I rarely did. When I was elected Queen of the Forestry Dance, I asked my dear friend Ray to take me, since I had no boyfriend. Ray was safe.

After two years at CSU, I transferred to Colorado Women's College. It was smaller and I didn't feel so much pressure to socialize. When I graduated, my father agreed to send me to graduate school.

I went as far away as I could, the University of Vienna. The old-world history of Austria and the Vienna Opera House captured my dreams and imagination. I studied political science and even learned to speak fluent German, not knowing then that learning a second language can be therapeutic for a person with a brain injury.

The process of learning the new language triggered the areas of my brain that dealt with memory and comprehension and improved my self-esteem.

I didn't completely heal while in Austria, but I grew stronger and I got a sense of what I wanted to do with my life.

I wanted to see the world, and I wanted to work and to feel useful.

I carried a terrible guilt because of my actions of crashing into the bridge, and from shame and struggles of the consequences of this choice. I had no understanding of why I would do such a self-destructive action. I never forgave myself, or understood until I was forty-eight years old the "why."

Guilt was the emotion I felt for what I had done. I covered it with my need for perfection to hide all the shame about what a bad person I thought I was. That shame ate away at my injured soul, until I finally forgave myself when I joined SUN years later, and realized the suicide attempt was actually a coping mechanism for children violated at a very young age by a person of trust.

I came up with a plan. After my studies, I would be a flight attendant for Pan American.

As I read about their program, I grew excited about the prospect of that career. Technically, my brain injury would be disqualifying, but there was no way for them to easily uncover my medical history. This was well before the Internet. So, when I submitted my application, I omitted any reference to the brain injury.

It never occurred to me I wouldn't get the job. I was supremely qualified, and my fluency in another language set me apart from the other women who applied. For the first time in my life, I was confident about my future.

I returned to Denver from Vienna, with an advanced degree in political science and a sense of purpose. I went to the Pan Am interview in a downtown Denver hotel lobby. I walked in confidently, wearing a smart skirt and heels. I gave the representative my credentials and talked about my time in Austria. The man seemed to like me. He laughed when I made a joke. He was impressed with my ability to speak German. I was certain I would be offered the position.

I was wrong.

However, life had taught me to keep going. **Nothing had ever turned out exactly the way I thought it should, yet my life had marched on despite the setbacks.** When I had struggled to pass classes, I hadn't given up. I had found a new way to study.

When Pan Am rejected me, I also did not give up. Failure was not an option.

I applied a second time with Pan Am and, again, I walked away feeling like the interview was a success. I knew my qualifications were excellent. Yet, again, I was turned down. Why? What was I missing? What was I doing wrong?

When they rejected me a third time, I decided to get to the bottom of things. I marched into the lobby of that hotel in downtown Denver and demanded that someone tell me what I was doing wrong. I waved my application papers under the nose of one of the recruiters and insisted that he look at it and tell me what was missing. I pointed out that I met or exceeded every qualification for the job. What else could they possibly want from an applicant? How was I not enough?

Most of the people there in the lobby refused to tell me anything. They waved me away with vague excuses about how there were only so many positions available. It was really frustrating.

Finally, one man noticed my determination and pulled me aside to tell me the truth.

"You are qualified," he said. "You're just what we're looking for, except for one thing; your face. We can't hire someone who looks like you," he said. "Our customers wouldn't like it."

The map of scars across my face.

I had forgotten. I had grown used to it. I had accepted them as part of me, no one ever said anything.

Pan Am had disqualified me from the job I wanted, and I had no Plan B. I had decided to work for them. I was determined to work for them no matter what I had to do.

I could have given up. I could have settled for a different job, one that didn't require me to work with the public. I could have cried or complained about how unfair it was. I didn't do any of these things.

My father's motto was, **"There is no problem that doesn't have a solution."**

I took his words to heart. If these scars were the only thing standing between me and the job I wanted, I would do something about it. I thanked the man for his honesty and promptly made an appointment with a good plastic surgeon. My father paid.

After months of resurfacing and healing, my face was nearly smooth. With a bit of foundation and the right blush, it was impossible to see the scars.

I took my new face back to that hotel where Pan Am was again recruiting. I handed them my credentials. I smiled. I was poised. I sailed through the interview, and got the job. **It's hard to beat someone who never gives up.**

# 2

# New Beginnings

## Pan Am to Creedmoor

Flying around the world as a stewardess with Pan Am, I saw places many people only dream about.

I was living in New York City with three other flight attendants and working with the flight crew in a confident and efficient manner. Passengers quickly learned that I knew what they needed before they asked. All the pride and satisfaction I had felt working summer jobs in Aspen, Colorado, came back to me.

It was the mid-1960s and the world was changing. Vietnam War protests were escalating, and the Civil Rights movement in was in full swing. We were no longer the placid, optimistic country of the 1950s.

I was changing, too. I was no longer the docile, scared little girl I had been. For the first time in my life, I was living on my own terms and this built in me an incredible, undaunted spirit to keep connected.

I faced my new life as an airline stewardess with determination and enthusiasm. I worked hard and tried to be the best at my job. I loved it, and I loved the hard work.

Air travel was still something of a luxury. The airlines were conscious of their public image and worked hard to set themselves apart for the customers who could afford to fly. Some of their best customers were powerful men who flew for business. They were courted with cocktails, steak dinners, and pretty flight attendants to bring them whatever they required. Advertisements in those days featured young, beautiful women in short skirts, offering coffee with a wink and a smile. We weren't called flight attendants then. We were stewardesses and we lived to serve.

With the sexual revolution in full swing, we were encouraged to show a little leg and to "be friendly." We were still expected to be "good." It was a fine line to walk. I was determined to be perfect at my job. I dressed the part. I smiled. I worked hard. I was good. I loved my job and the opportunity to see the world and meet people in New York. If I did not work on the weekend I would go to a wedding at the big hotels or I would attend a Bar Mitzvah at the large Synagogues. I was never invited but it was the only chance to meet decent people. I did not go to bars, instead creating an opportunity as a young woman. That is the way I met the wonderful people of New York, the city I love so much.

On Thursday nights, my friends and I would try to beat the trash pickup on Friday morning and get some of the furniture and items the residents threw away. That is how we furnished our apartment.

Many of my coworkers dated men they met while working. Some got married and for many women that was the ultimate goal. Marriage meant the end of the career, but that was okay as the airlines didn't want to employ women after a certain age.

I went on a few dates, but it wasn't easy for me. All those years of being told by my mother that I wasn't good enough had left its mark. My brothers' violence and humiliation had left me fearful of interacting with men. I wanted a family, but I wasn't sure I wanted a husband.

Thankfully, my work kept me too busy to dwell on the doubts that filled my mind. I embraced my role as a Pan Am stewardess and I threw myself into my job. I was fascinated by a city that offered so many opportunities – from the opera to the museums, bicycle riding in central park, eating lunch where the taxi drivers ate, and even riding the old wooden escalators at Macy's department store. It was a thrilling time to live in New York.

I also found a way to be useful.

Pan Am and many other airlines participated in an airline volunteer program called Dooley Intermed International. Flight attendants and crew members were encouraged to volunteer in remote locations, many ravaged by war, poverty, and natural disasters. Volunteers were granted three months of unpaid leave to provide humanitarian aid at orphanages, health clinics, schools, and communities in India, Nepal, Vietnam, Laos, and Thailand.

I worked alongside doctors, nurses, and teachers to bring fresh food and water, health care and education to people who needed it. It was very satisfying to me to make a small contribution.

The media covered the mission trips and called the army of volunteer flight attendants Dooley's Dollies. It was the PR for the airlines—we were the ultimate in airline ambassadors.

I volunteered at an orphanage in Kathmandu, where I discovered Nepal, Buddhist temples, ancient archaeological ruins, deeply forested lush green landscapes, abundant fruit trees, farmers living simple productive lives working in fields of rice and wheat, and mountains and pathways that reminded me of Aspen, Colorado, where I had spent much of my childhood.

Being in Nepal gave my life a deep sense of fulfillment and meaning. Yet, this also was a volatile political climate. Until the 1950s, they had almost no access to medical care or schools. Infrastructure for roads and modern utilities were nonexistent. Poverty was a way of life, and hunger a pressing issue.

I assisted nurses with healthcare tasks. I helped staff prepare good, healthy food. I taught classes and sang with the children.

It was a special time. The resilience of the Nepalese children was amazing. They had lost their parents and their homes, but they were happy and full of life. In my three months at the orphanage, I grew to know many of them and loved them dearly.

**To my surprise, my own struggles were diminished. I realized the more you lose yourself in something bigger than yourself, the more energy you will have.** I began to imagine having children of my own. I hadn't yet met a man I could fathom marrying, but I now understood the appeal of motherhood. I had seen the difference I was making at the orphanage, and I loved watching the children learn and watching them grow stronger each day.

My own struggles were diminished as I poured my energy and my love into helping these children heal. How could I not hope to feel that every day?

Even after my volunteer assignment was over, my heart remained with the orphaned children. As I fell asleep each night, I saw their smiling faces and I felt their small hands tugging at me.

As a Pan Am volunteer, I had witnessed the enormous and inspiring examples of the human spirit wrapped up in these young children. I dreamed of the day I could return and see them again.

If these abandoned children could survive and thrive, then, I realized, we are all capable of more than we imagine. **If these orphans could find happiness in mundane activities and see beauty in the world around them, then the rest of us can do the same.**

They made their life happy, even though it was very hard.

I loved all the children I worked with, but the little girls inspired me the most. They were small and seemingly fragile. Alone in the world, they had every excuse to be sad and scared. Once I got to know them, I saw nothing other than their immense strength and spirit.

These girls were survivors. They didn't sink into depression or focus on the injustice of their circumstances. Instead, they embraced life and learned to adapt. They were like the Himalayan Cypress trees: strong but flexible enough to withstand the most destructive of winds. They knew when to stand firm. They knew how to let the storms of life roll over them.

The Nepalis have a saying: **"Blessed are the flexible, for they shall not be bent out of shape."**

Those children inspired me.

Back in New York City in the late 1960s, Pan Am Flight 485 hosted an all female soccer publicity match at Yankee Stadium, airline stewardesses vs. the Playboy Bunnies, dozens of young women running up and down the field in skimpy tops and short shorts. Interviews on radio, television, and billboards throughout the city hyped the match.

Only the most athletic participated. My wreck at age sixteen had erased my Olympic dream but not my athletic prowess.

I had regained some of my former speed and stamina. I still enjoyed the feeling of running hard and fast, and I still liked the thrill of competition. So, I looked forward to the Pan Am soccer match.

Denice - PanAm

It was exciting to enter Yankee Stadium and hear the crowd roar as we moved the ball up and down the field on that beautiful summer day.

With sweat rolling down my face and my lungs taking in the hot air, I kicked the soccer ball to a coworker and ran. Then a girl on the other team slammed me into the stadium wall. My head thumped and bounced against the wall. I seized, fell to the ground, and contorted violently.

Medics ran onto the field and carried me away on a stretcher.

At the hospital, I was put into a medically induced coma to keep my brain from swelling. I was brought to the New York Hospital. Then I was transferred to Creedmoor asylum since the hospital was unable to control my seizures.

With my hands over my ears, I tried to sleep, but nothing could drown out the tortured screams of the other patients. I didn't know where I was. I was completely disoriented. It was unsettling to know it was no longer summer, but late fall. When I was placed at Creedmoor Asylum, 8,000 mental patients were housed there. That was the dumping ground when the hospital beds were needed, and they were unable to treat a patient successfully with medication. The hospital was unable to stop the seizures I was having, and the Dr. in charge of my case was frustrated by this, so he gave me 800mg of Thorazine (twice the threshold limit). Thorazine would sometimes have the opposite effect of what it was prescribed for, and would lower the seizure threshold. This is what happened to me.

Thirty years later, Dr. Gregory Wilets, working on a custody evaluation for me stated, "The 800mg of Thorazine they gave me, would have been considered poor treatment, and for anybody who has taken Thorazine it's an awful experience, it increases the likelihood of seizures and could have been causing deterioration in her condition."

The atmosphere at Creedmoor was constant noise and screaming day and night. This was a warehouse of humanity, watched over by some of the most perverted workers, or "Therapy Aids." These minimum wage employees took their frustration out on the patients. They used excessive restraints, including straight jackets to control us. While restrained, the patients would have to beg to use the restroom. Many times, the request would be dismissed, and the patient had no recourse but to lie in their own urine and feces.

This further degraded and humiliated patients and kept them in a powerless position They would give us pharmaceuticals to keep us docile and compliant. I was given a much higher dose than recommended of Thorazine 4 times /day, even though (as stated earlier) it will often have the opposite effect than intended for people with seizures and lowers the seizure threshold. Thorazine is now discontinued, and although the generic form is still available, it is rarely prescribed.

Neglect was a way of life, and the norm at Creedmoor. I knew I did not belong there, and with the way it was run, neither did anyone else. I got to know some of the poor souls who had lived in this "House of

Horrors" far longer than I had, and none of them deserved this treatment. If I had to choose between the staff and the patients, I would choose the patients because at least they were not deliberately cruel. One of the most popular treatments at the asylum was Electroshock Therapy. I watched patients return drooling and unable to speak and then be tied to a chair to keep from sliding to the floor. My only blessing during that time was the note on my chart about my brain injury. Although it made me a bad candidate for Electroshock Therapy, I was still lucid enough to watch every despicable moment. I witnessed numerous examples of violence. I saw some of the staff physically abuse and molest the patients. I myself experienced this when I was put in a straitjacket by an aide who verbally ridiculed me while he masturbated. My depression returned. Creedmoor was severely underfunded, overcrowded, and understaffed.

It was well on its way to becoming the infamous New York Institution that was the subject of documentaries. Patients were restricted to the ward, and never even allowed to go outside. The hopelessness of Creedmoor permeated patient's thoughts, so that it was easy to believe that this place was their plight for the rest of their life. A few years after my stay at Creedmoor, the hospital was the site of a two-year outbreak of violence. This outbreak included multiple rapes, dozens of assaults, over fifty fires, several suicides, a shooting, and at least one attempted murder.

The previous summer I was on the top of the world, working for Pan Am. Now I found myself on the floor of an asylum, humiliated and degraded, relegated to the lowest form of a human being.

Luckily my father knew my spirit, and never gave up on me. He paid a psychiatrist a great deal of money to assume responsibility for me at a private hospital in Denver, ending my nightmare, and "getting me out of the system."

My experiences gave me a very frightened perspective of how cruel life could actually be. I tucked the experience away, and never forgot. It gave me a determination to live a successful life. I was empowered by the fear and horror of Creedmoor.

Instead of "poor me", I realized it was "strong me." You can lose complete control of your life yet come back so strong that you only want to create the best possible future. Freedom is the power to make our own changes, take our own risks, and not have our lives be dictated by others. I found joy in every moment of my new freedom.

I appreciated my father's efforts and never forgot his support and belief that I would go forward – he always told me, **"Getting knocked down in life happens, getting up is your choice."** You can not start the next chapter of your life if you keep rereading the last. My memories of

Creedmoor became my most painful blessings and motivation. I didn't remember everything that happened to me there, but I didn't forget. Regardless of the horror, I was determined to do better and not let my darkest experience define me as a victim. **I knew I had hit the lowest point in my life, yet was determined to learn from my past and not let the experiences define my future. I was protective of my new-found freedom, and very cautious while navigating this new life.**

# 3

# Demons Come with Smiles

## Betrayal Creates a Stronger Woman

After returning to Denver, I convinced myself that marrying the doctor who had pursued me was the right decision. I returned to Denver to start my new life. **Never make a life decision in a vulnerable state.**

From the beginning of our married life, he was often highly critical of me. Sometimes he was sweet, most times, he spoke harshly. His inability to handle little things—a flat tire, getting lost, any mild annoyance—was the tip of the iceberg.

He questioned my intelligence and insulted me, he would use confusing lies and projections. He even threatened, "I'm a doctor, I could easily put you back in the asylum." He stabbed at my most vulnerable, painful secret, and used it as an opportunity to control me. My childhood abuse had made sharp remarks familiar.

I told myself that my new husband and I had our whole lives to get to know each other. I was not a quitter, and perhaps we could learn to love one another. I would take the good with the bad. I was often confused by these lies and projections. It was as if I had lost my ability to think. Everything was always my fault, while he protected himself with layer upon layer of self-deception. He had been betrayed by his parents, and his first wife. I didn't realize at the time, but it is impossible to remove the previous stain(s) of betrayal from someone else's life. I began to realize it is hard to remove someone's feelings of victimhood - which motivates their entire life. They will always be a martyr.

Over the next few months, I got to know his family, including his daughter from his first marriage. Maura was four and very needy from being shuttled back and forth between her parents. She was confused and frightened. I was a stranger and I was always with her father.

He and I tried to explain to her that we were getting married.

She cried a lot.

It was stressful to be around her, but I looked forward to having my own children, so I worked to build a solid relationship with her. I wanted to be a good mother.

In retrospect, it would have been a good idea to learn more about the reasons my husband's first marriage had failed. I could have saved myself years of unhappiness. I only had his side of the story.

He'd said his first wife was unstable and he blamed her for the failure of the marriage. **I should have been wary of a person who always blamed others.**

He never believed anything was his fault.

No responsibility was ever taken for his actions or the consequences that followed. He was a man, powerful and privileged—a doctor.

I think my injuries and my terrible time in Creedmoor are what attracted him to me. I was someone to control, someone who was vulnerable in his eyes.

Just before we married, he took Maura and me to the Continental Divide Racetrack for an afternoon of car racing. He was the doctor on call, which allowed him to watch from restricted areas, including the pits where the cars came and went. It was loud and exciting in some ways to be so close to the action. It also turned out to be terribly dangerous.

Maura wailed and then melted into a full temper tantrum. My fiancé was furious with me because I couldn't soothe her. He picked her up and stormed off—and that's when a car flew off the racetrack. Two people in the pits were killed, the man standing next to me, and the race car driver.

Somehow, I survived. The next thing I remember, I was riding in an ambulance and wondering where all the blood was coming from.

My fiancé was in the ambulance, too, but he was riding up front, not in the back with me. I heard him talking to the ambulance driver, making jokes and bragging about his professional accomplishments to impress them with his "importance." I thought I must be imagining it, because it was so inappropriate.

The debris from the crash struck me on the left side of my face and scalp, resulting in 136 stitches, and injuries to my left side.

The miracle of survival was something I was getting used to. I should have seen that accident as a sign of things to come.

Race Track Accident 1969

It didn't occur to me then to call off the wedding. Quitting is not what I do. Whenever things were tough, I kept going. Besides, everyone would be disappointed.

I convinced myself everything would be fine. Women became wives every day. If they could do it, I could, too. We are all always one decision away from a totally different life.

Our wedding was in August at Temple Emmanuel in Denver. We'd planned to spend our honeymoon in Aspen, where I'd spent so much of my time as a child and where I'd had my happiest years. I looked forward to returning. Aspen still felt like home to me, and my parents still owned property there. I wanted to show off Aspen to my new husband. I wanted him to understand why I loved the town so much.

We drove to the mountains in my great aunt's old powder blue, big-finned DeSoto. It was like driving a large couch down the highway.

We had a flat tire on the way up the mountain, the first of many bad moments on the trip. My husband had never changed a tire. My father had taught me, so I did it.

As I struggled to break the seal on the lug nuts, my husband refused to help. "We're stranded!" he screamed, freaking out. "On this narrow mountain road!"

I couldn't understand his hysteria. "It's just a flat tire," I said. "Easily fixed."

"We're going to die! It's your fault! We should have brought my car ... not this old junker!"

How could he treat patients with such temperament? How could he be a physician?

Sweating and covered in dirt, I got the tire changed—and remained silent.

As we continued up the mountain, I hoped my husband's meltdown was an anomaly. It wasn't.

One afternoon, we went for a motorbike ride. I wanted to show him the trail where my family and I used to hike.

Aspen had changed, though. It seemed like a different town. There were more houses, roads and buildings, and signs I didn't recognize. Aspen was no longer a sleepy mining town with the miners, shop owners, and ranchers all living as equals. It was becoming a posh resort destination.

I couldn't find the trail and we came upon a bridge that had washed out over a river, so we had to backtrack with our motorbikes. It was a warm day, and we were both tired.

"Dragging me here was a fool's errand!" my husband exploded.

"It's a beautiful day and we're on our honeymoon," I said optimistically. "It's an adventure, something we can laugh about with our grandchildren."

Back home after the misadventure, I was starting to feel physically sick and nauseous.

"My parents are bringing Maura home," my husband said to me, "and you need to cook for them and entertain."

Despite not feeling like myself, I cooked and pretended to eat in front of his family. I was determined to be a good hostess, though I had no appetite, and I was overwhelmed with nausea.

The next day, I told him, "I'm sick. I need to see a doctor." "You're fine. Stop worrying. It's nothing," he replied.

Nevertheless, I found a doctor through the yellow pages, and he ran some tests.

Soon, he reported to me, "You're pregnant."

"We'll tell everyone it's a preemie," my mother said. She was a good example of the women of that generation. She lived in total denial of reality, and was consumed with the importance of people's opinions.

You can never wake someone up who pretends to be asleep. My mother lived a fantasized reality.

My husband was rarely home. He was always on the golf course, only occasionally working at the hospital. It was a very isolating atmosphere. Many of the other doctors' wives were surviving this isolation with the help of volunteering as a Pink Lady at the hospital, shopping, alcohol, or therapy.

I was always cautious around these people and just tried to blend into that life. I started going to estate sales to earn extra money.

Just after we were married, Maura came to live with us full time. She was four, and her own mother wanted to "start over", so was signing away her rights to her daughter. It was unheard of for a mother to sign away rights to her child, but she did so, and never looked back.

My husband said, "Taking care of children is the wife's job, and you are the wife, I am the one saving lives."

She was very needy and demanding, and it became a 24hour/day job to fulfill her needs. Just a few years earlier, I'd had a successful career, flying all over the world, earning my own money. I was independent and lived in an apartment in New York City. It was a very happy time.

Now, I was mother to an unhappy child. The first year of marriage was supposed to be good, yet I often cried myself to sleep.

Around that time, I read an article by Thomas Maeder titled, "Wounded Healers," it was about physicians, who chose their profession not to help others but to help themselves, and that they suffer from a **God Complex, "characterized by aloofness, inaccessibility, and mysteriousness," that many are narcissists who worry more about the appearance of their lives than the reality. They aren't ethical, though they put forth an image of moral superiority. They seek relationships with people they can manipulate and exploit. In marriage, they are distant, cold, and unaffectionate. They choose spouses who are vulnerable, dependent, and emotionally troubled, someone to help them feel superior and provide the admiration they require."**

I recognized this in my husband, and in my marriage.

Fortunately for me (and unfortunately for him) my vulnerable weakness was a temporary state, and I was able to minimize his ugly behavior and no longer let his negativity run my life. I no longer felt his insults, because I had learned to not value his opinions.

In the late stages of my pregnancy, I was nesting. I wanted to get our home ready for the new baby. I painted walls and rearranged the furniture. I cleaned. I had the carpet replaced. I was a woman on a mission.

One day when some workmen were scheduled to arrive, I asked my husband to move the refrigerator out of their way for me.

"I'm late for my tee time. I can't do it," he replied

So, after he left, I squatted in front of the appliance and grabbed on with both hands, thinking how hard could it be? I pulled and pulled. It moved an inch. I pulled again, sweating, and panting, my back aching. Though dizzy, I took a deep breath, squatted lower and pulled on the refrigerator with all my might.

I felt blood between my legs. Only then did I realize I may have hurt my unborn child. Immediately, I called my husband. "I'm bleeding. I need to go to the hospital!" He arrived to take me to the hospital, and instead of concerned, he was angry.

He yelled, "You should never have tried to move something so heavy, How could you be so stupid?"

I let his insults wash over me. I was very frightened and was only focusing on my unborn child.

The doctors took me into delivery—but for four days, nothing happened. They couldn't figure out what was wrong, and decided to take some x-rays (even though ultrasound was invented, it still was not commonly used).

The decision was made to perform a C-Section.

I felt like a specimen on the table, naked and exposed. I felt ashamed.

Then the drugs kicked in and everything went black.

During the procedure, the stress triggered a series of violent seizures.

The doctors kept me sedated for three days after my baby was born. When I was finally aware of my surroundings, the nurses were quiet, too quiet.

"Where's my baby?" I asked a nurse. She didn't answer. She just scurried out of the room to get a doctor.

"Where's my baby?" I asked him when he arrived.

He took my hand. "It was a difficult birth. You'll never have another child."

"Please", I said, "Take me to my child."

He answered, "She's in intensive care. She only weighs a pound-and-a-half. She's jaundiced and her tiny lungs are struggling to pump oxygen through her body. It's a miracle she's alive."

It took me a few minutes to understand. She wasn't breathing when she was born.

"We thought she was a stillbirth," he continued, "She was blue when we first pulled her out. We almost gave up on reviving her." Then he smiled and said, "But we saved her."

I cried, "Thank you."

He helped me into a wheelchair and off we went. I met Michelle for the first time, so tiny and fragile, and so beautiful.

Her skin was golden from the jaundice, her lips opening and closing, like a baby bird gasping for food as she struggled to live.

I loved her immediately and fiercely.

"She's so small," I said to the doctor.

"She could suffer a number of problems. She might be blind. She might have trouble learning. She might not develop at the rate of other children." He paused. "We don't really know. We just don't know."

But when I looked at Michelle's beautiful face, I knew she was going to be okay. No matter what, she was perfect, and I would care for her. I would make her strong. I would pour every ounce of energy I had into helping her be well and whole. I am forever grateful to the Pediatrician, Dr. Ray Rademacher, for his decision to save her.

It was hours before I realized no one knew where my husband was. He had not been there for the past four days.

When he did come see me later, he said, "I couldn't stay here, looking at her, and the doctors saying you'll never have another child. It was just too much. All too disappointing. I couldn't put myself through it."

After I got home, Michelle remained in the hospital for a few months. I went to see her every day, watching her develop and thrive. My husband's daughter went with me during those visits because my husband would not help with her care. Not only was he the invisible husband, but he was also the invisible father.

Acceptance of his behavior made my life easier.

"It isn't supposed to be like this," he would dramatically whine. I paid no attention, as I was so thrilled to have Michelle.

After I was discharged, I worked hard to please him, as I had my mother and brothers when I was a child. I craved his approval but realized I could never make him happy.

I began to think of him as my adversary, always negative while I strived to be positive. In public, he pretended things were perfect. At home he barked demands, complained, and blamed me for everything that went wrong.

I began to dread spending time alone with him. **He was not Prince Charming, I now saw him as the "Prince of Darkness."** He thought the world revolved around him. I started referring to him as "*The Prince*" around the children, secretly knowing what I really meant was, "*The*

*Prince* of Darkness." It was a terrible feeling to realize I was sleeping with the enemy.

Still, I had gotten what I wanted. I was a mother. And despite the warnings from the doctors, Michelle thrived.

She developed into a healthy, beautiful girl. Her resilience reminded me of the children in the orphanage in Nepal, who always found beauty in the world and made my heart sing.

Even as an infant, she showed tremendous spirit and spunk. It was clear that I had nothing but gratitude, and that she had blessed my life in every way possible. Once again I felt I was so lucky, it felt like I had won the lottery….this time, the Mega Lottery.

Home with Michelle, my life finally felt complete.

"Take a photo of me with the baby," I asked *The Prince*, because I wanted to preserve this moment.

He shrugged and left the room. So, I took Michelle and walked down our alley. I introduced myself to a neighbor who was working in his garage, "Can you take a picture of me and my new baby?", I asked.

The neighbor was John Battles, a highly decorated World War 2 pilot, and he went and got his wife, Lizzy, and she took the photo. Their enthusiasm at being asked to document this special event warmed my heart, and from that moment on we were dear friends. It was a very precious time.

John and Lizzy Battles

After that, John, Lizzie, and me often spent weekends together, visiting neighborhood garage sales, hunting for treasures. We laughed a lot, and our friendship developed into the first unconditional love I had felt since my father had passed. For years on April Fools' Day, I woke them at six a.m. "There's an amazing garage sale we have to visit!" When they arrived there, I greeted them with a sign, Happy April Fools!

Another time, I had someone call them claiming to be an IRS agent threatening an audit. I showed up at my friends' house that day and found John on the phone with the actual IRS, determined to straighten things out. I laughed as I told him the truth, and he melted with relief.

One year, I bought a tree removal notice for Dutch Elm trees from the Forestry Department because John and Lizzy had huge elms in their yard. I marked their trunks with tempera paint, then sent the Dutch Elm notice to their house via certified mail. John went straight to the Forestry Department to try and save his trees. An official told him, "Your trees are American Elm, and you'll do well to learn the difference."

Luckily for me, John and Lizzy loved my pranks and loved me. They always swore they would get me back the next year, but they never did. They only helped me. They were always ready to lend a hand.

Once when I was playing "Hide and Seek" with my children, I climbed a cherry tree in my yard and, somehow, got my bra stuck on a branch. I couldn't let go of the tree without falling, and I couldn't get my bra unstuck without letting go of the branch. I yelled to the children, "Call John! Tell him I'm up a tree and I can't get down."

John and Lizzy rushed right over. He held onto my feet while I struggled with my bra and finally made it down. We all doubled over with laughter.

As Michelle grew older, she often ran down the alley to visit the Battles. Lizzy would call to let me know Michelle was with her and I would tell her not to give Michelle too much candy. They loved spoiling her. Lizzy's mother, Hazel, was living with them at the time. Michelle couldn't pronounce "Hazel," so she called her "Hassle." We would

John walking Michelle down the aisle on the river at the Aspen house, in the dress and bouquet I made

often find Michelle asleep on "Hassle's" lap. The Battles became like Michelle's grandparents, especially after my mother also passed away. **It was a relationship of unconditional love.** We included the Battles in all our important life events. John even walked Michelle down the aisle at her wedding. They were my dearest friends for forty years, until they both passed. The memory of them still makes my heart smile.

My mother-in-law came and stayed for a few weeks when Michelle was two months old. She was a big help. She made sure I got some sleep while she watched Maura and Michelle, though she refused to give Michelle a bath. "She's too tiny!", she would say.

We both laughed about how nervous she was. After all, she had birthed and raised two children herself. "But I've never seen a baby as tiny and delicate as Michelle," she said.

My own parents stopped by several times to visit and fawn over their granddaughter. My mother treasured Michelle, often bringing peppermint ice cream and pretty dresses.

Everyone loved Michelle. I had tried for so long to be the perfect daughter, the perfect sister, the perfect wife.

Even though *The Prince* said he was smitten with our daughter, he never helped with diapers or feedings. Because of her low birth weight, she woke up every ninety minutes to be fed. He never helped. Instead, he scheduled even more days of golf. I didn't mind his absence, except when I needed help. **It was always more relaxing without him there.**

Once his mother left, I was on my own with my infant and the now five-year-old Maura, who was not thrilled about the new baby. She had been the only child. She had seen her parents split up. She had been shuttled from her mother's house to our house. She must have wondered if the new baby would take her place. She lashed out in tantrums and acted out to get attention, sometimes regressing while eating or talking, other times flying into violent rages.

It was about this time that *The Prince's* uncle called and asked me for a favor for his daughter.

"Jill is nineteen and she's had a rough couple of years. She's fallen in with a bad crowd and got hooked on drugs. We've tried to deal with it ourselves, but we can't help her. She was arrested in Cleveland for possession of heroin. She could go to jail. Because she is young, the judge offered her probation if she will stay clean and out of trouble. She needs a fresh start in a new town, away from the friends and drugs that got her into trouble in the first place. Could she come live with you? The judge has already signed off on the arrangement. He was impressed that your husband is a doctor and said that might be good for Jill."

"I can't make that decision on my own."

I stated, "I'll have to talk to my husband about it."

He then let me know that my husband had already agreed that Jill could come.

That night, I argued with *The Prince*. "How could you do this without consulting me? How am I supposed to raise Maura, care for an infant, and run a household while keeping a constant eye on a drug addict?"

"It's already decided. You have to make it work, " he said. Maybe she could help out around the house."

Jill's arrival did not make things easier with Maura or my life with a new infant.

Because of my own rough teen years, I wanted to help Jill. It was hard because she lied about everything. I tried to understand.

I helped her secure a job at the local drugstore and tried to be a positive influence. Keeping track of her was a losing battle. When I tried to talk with *The Prince* about Jill, he just ignored me.

All of her "friends" looked like trouble as well. When they dropped by to pick her up, I asked a lot of questions.

*The Prince* later told me, "Back off."

"But I have a bad feeling. I think Jill is still doing drugs," I answered. "Don't worry so much," he said. "You're being ridiculous."

My instincts said Jill was trouble.

I should have trusted them. It was a complete fluke that I saw a letter addressed to Jill arrive.

Something didn't feel right, so I opened it, and I could hardly believe what I read. Jill and her friends were conspiring to ship heroin through the mail.

I assumed she had been smoking marijuana, I knew that was unacceptable, but heroin was another matter. I had a baby in the house and a small child. I couldn't have heroin addicts coming around. I couldn't have a heroin addict living here any longer either.

Jill's probation required her to remain clean and sober. I now knew she wasn't. Worse, she was committing felonies while living under my roof. Her new friends were coming around more often, and I now knew it was very dangerous.

I called *The Prince*. "We have to do something."

"Don't worry about it. I'll handle it ... And must I remind you that opening another person's mail is also a felony offence? You could be arrested," was his only reply.

But he didn't do anything.

So, I finally contacted Jill's probation officer. He asked me to bring her to his office at the Federal Building in downtown Denver and tell her it was just a routine meeting.

So, as Jill and I were driving the next day, I told her, "It's a routine follow-up."

"I'm sure it's nothing," she said nonchalantly, "because I've done nothing wrong."

I marveled at her ability to lie.

At the Federal Building, Jill's probation was revoked, and she was arrested and taken to jail.

I did not feel guilt, she needed more help than I was able to give. I was hoping the arrest would be the first step toward getting her life in order. She needed to hit rock bottom, like I had at Creedmoor, to be able to lift herself into a new life.

When *The Prince* learned I had called her probation officer, he screamed at me. "I can't believe you went against my advice! You should have called her father first."

"He's in Ohio" I said. He hasn't seen her every day like I have. The way she lies, the people she's hanging around with."

That afternoon, two policemen showed up at our door. They asked me to sit down, and one said, "We have bad news. We're sorry … but Jill killed herself in her cell."

"I don't understand. How could this happen? It must be a mistake. I just dropped her off." I paused, "How?"

"She hung herself with her knee socks," he replied.

It was the 1970s. All young girls wore long socks with their skirts.

"In jail, they take away belts and ties," I said. "I guess they didn't think about the socks."

After the officers left, *The Prince* turned on me. "If you hadn't turned her in, she'd still be alive! You call her father. I won't touch it!"

I did as I was told.

I went to see Jill with Michelle and Maura, *the Prince* refused to help. Her head was wrapped in cellophane. It was heartbreaking. She had been a pretty girl, a bright girl. She was so young. She had so much potential.

I felt terrible for her father. He had done everything he knew to do and still she was gone. I had to take her remains to Cleveland in a small cardboard box. It was a very sad time. It was very unusual at the time to cremate if you were of the Jewish faith, but that was how sad of a time it was. He was distraught.

*The Prince* now became even more violent. Something was unleashed inside him. We put forth the image of domestic bliss, but behind closed doors our life was chaos. Nothing I did was ever enough. Whenever he lost his temper, and struck me – he always acted like he was the injured party. At first I thought I was to blame for him hitting me, it was confusing. Over time, I just stayed afraid, and walked on eggshells around him.

I knew in my heart that Jill was in a better place, no longer burdened with addiction, finally at peace. But there was no peace in my home.

"It's your fault!" *The Prince* would shout at me about Jill. He continued to blame me for everything that went wrong, big and small. If the baby cried, it was my fault. If Maura had a cold, it was my fault.

And I internalized the blame, just as I had as a child. I became silent.

One day when I was putting Michelle down for a nap, someone knocked at the back door and five year old Maura answered, even though I had taught her not to. Jill had a lot of friends who dealt drugs and were convicted felons. Some were violent. Even after she died, we'd had some shady characters show up at the back door, looking to score drugs.

I heard Maura yell, "I'll get it."

"Ask who it is," I said, and hurried to answer the door before her.

She ignored me and opened the door.

It was only my brother stopping by to fix a broken pipe in the basement, but I scolded her, bending down to say, "How many times do I have to tell you? It's dangerous."

"I checked who was there," she said.

It was a lie. I had seen the whole thing. "That isn't true. You always have to tell the truth," I told her.

She stomped her foot. "I'm not lying."

I wanted her to understand that lying has consequences. I feared for a child who doesn't tell the truth.

I couldn't let the lies with Maura stand. I had to make her understand how important it is to tell the truth. "Just tell me the truth," I said.

She screamed and cried in rage.

I grabbed her shoulders and made her look at me. "I only want the truth."

*The Prince* stomped downstairs from the third floor, yanked me away from Maura, reared back and struck me with the back of his hand. The force landed me on top of the washing machine.

I was shocked, though I shouldn't have been. *The Prince* was always unpredictable. Verbally, he lashed out at me all the time. My brother witnessed the whole thing but said nothing.

Big brothers are supposed to protect their little sisters, but with my brother, it was the opposite, maybe because he didn't want to acknowledge his own dark secrets with me.

Even, nineteen years later, when I was contemplating divorce, my brother said, "Don't divorce him. Don't leave him. look at what you've become because of him. You have a comfortable life," implying it was a fine trade-off and that I never could have succeeded on my own. Long ago I accepted this lack of support from my family (except for my father, who always supported me). As soon as I accepted that reality of this betrayal, it was easier.

This was the first time *The Prince* had hit me in front of anyone. In that moment, as I looked at his face, which was twisted in anger and hatred, it all became clear.

Maura stopped crying as she stared at him, then back at me. I could see her calculating her role in the incident. Her screams had brought her father running. Now she knew how to get his attention. From that moment on, she took any chance she could to cause chaos and force him to swoop in and rescue her. This became her coping skills for dealing with the traumas of her own life. If children do not learn that bad behavior is not tolerated at a young age, then it will be something they are never able to learn.

In the midst of all this, Michelle cried.

I stood up, tall. "I'm going to check on the baby." At that moment, I no longer trusted him.

I left the room with all the dignity I could.

Soon after, he tried to make things right. He was tender to me. He sent me flowers. "You should try to get some rest," he said. "I love you."

But I was wary of him now. I no longer trusted him. He would strike again. This was a life-changing event for me. I became indifferent to his belittling and rage. I started to plan my life without him being part of it. He completely broke my trust. Our marriage was like a broken vase..... in pieces. You try to glue the shattered pieces together, but the original is gone, and a weaker version is in its place. **You can still put the glued vase back on the shelf, with the part that is not broken showing, but it is now worthless.**

I visited our rabbis. "I'm afraid of my husband," I told them.

The older rabbi had known him since he was a child. "He's a good man from a good family. He would never do something like that."

The younger rabbi admitted, "I have heard of his temper at the hospital, but I dismissed the possibility he would ever hurt you."

I was just a housewife who had married a violent man. I would have to live with the consequences. *The Prince* had a dark side that was well hidden in the never questioned status afforded to doctors at that time.

After that, whenever *The Prince* and I attended synagogue as a family, I smiled and sat with my daughters as if everything were normal. I had learned to compartmentalize my disappointment and look at the bigger picture. I loved being with the girls and enjoyed every other aspect of my life. I knew he was having affairs, because he would always try to get me to fight with him – then he would rationalize these fights were why he was having affairs. After I learned his game, I never reacted again. I just didn't care. He chose to disrespect me, but I had become strong and no longer gave him permission to destroy my spirit.

When you have learned to wear blinders in private, and a mask in public, life is hard. I had too much to give up.

**Sometimes being strong is the only option. I learned to walk away from his betrayals, and began to accept the unacceptable, knowing someday I would develop the courage to leave the marriage.**

**If you are in a hole, don't keep digging – change your behavior.**

# 4

# It's Hard to Beat Someone Who Never Gives Up

## Adoption to the Real Estate Exam

enjoyed being a mother, and was determined to have another baby, so I started to explore adoption.

I had struggled with Maura when she came into my life at four. It had been difficult to win her trust and affection. I felt I needed a newborn, a baby who would never know any other mother but me. I wanted another chance to be a mother.

Adoption in the 1970s was very difficult. There were no overseas adoptions, and the wait for healthy American babies was very long and defeating.

"We have enough to deal with," *The Prince* complained. But I talked him into going to an adoption agency with me anyway.

As we sat there, I was stunned that prospective parents were ruled out for almost any reason: religion, race, health history, or income.

"You already have two children," the woman told us, "and you aren't as young as most parents who are looking to adopt. Those factors alone make it unlikely that you will be approved."

However, I didn't give up.

A private adoption might be a solution, I decided. I just had to find the right woman, one who was willing to surrender her child to me. It wasn't uncommon, although it wasn't legal.

Being married to a doctor, I knew the medical community. I reached out to a gynecologist I thought would be sympathetic.

"Do you ever see women who want to give up their babies?" I asked him.

"All the time," he answered.

We talked about how it would work. He would call me when he had a woman who might be a good prospect. I met some of them and even paid some of their bills in advance. But I quickly learned that a woman who says she doesn't want to raise a baby might change her mind once that baby is born. Time and time again I got my hopes up, only to have the mother pull out of the agreement at the last minute. Although I was disappointed, I had empathy for the women who were making such a huge decision.

The gynecologist would call me to report on women who wanted to surrender their babies, thirteen times over a period of three years. I drove to the hospital and waited in the parking lot after the babies were born. I waited for the new mothers to walk out of the hospital and hand their baby over to me personally. That's what was required. They had to willingly surrender their baby, and not inside the hospital.

Also, any woman who agreed to this private adoption had to hold her newborn baby to her chest, listen to it cry, inhale the new baby scent and feel the tiny flutter of the heartbeat before handing her baby over to me.

Thirteen times I left empty-handed. Thirteen times I waited in the parking lot, praying the woman would follow through with the adoption.

These were women who would have a hard time raising their baby. They didn't have the money or resources. I hoped a woman would see my good intentions. I would love her baby as my own.

I was so determined that even *The Prince* stopped fighting me.

Finally, on my fourteenth trip to the hospital, a woman came out with her baby. On that trip, my attorney, Jerry Kay, was with me. The mother surrendered her newborn to him. He then handed the tiny infant to me. This kept me from meeting the mother, which could have legal implications.

On that trip, as all the rest, I was prepared. I had brought a bassinet, and I placed the tiny newborn in it and wrapped her with blankets for the trip home.

Kay was another beautiful baby girl for me to love. My heart nearly burst as I counted her tiny fingers and toes. Her face was like a Gerber baby. Just like when I first saw Michelle. My heart was overwhelmed with love and bonding – there was no difference. I had waited so long for Kay, it was a thrilling moment in my life.

After all the fights with *The Prince*, being told I was too old or too damaged, and after all my troubles with Maura, I had succeeded. I had another baby. **I was a Mommy once again and so very pleased to have her touch our lives in so many ways.**

I took my girls with me everywhere. It was 1974.

Maura was nine Michelle had just turned four, and Kay was the perfect infant. I took them all to the estate sales I would buy items to resell at my own yard sale. Those were wonderful times. Also it was needed. My children needed food, clothing, braces, and good schools, and I was happy to provide these things. I provided it.

After awhile it was no longer practical to sell the items from the front yard, so I rented a space at one of the antique malls, at 1420 South Broadway in Denver. There I displayed the glassware and fragile items to prospective buyers. I became known especially for my collection of restored antique dolls.

My mother had had an old doll and I had taken it to a repair shop in town. It needed a little TLC and a new dress. When I got the doll back, I was disappointed with the workmanship. The new dress was cheap polyester, and the repairs were poorly done.

I can do better than that, I thought. And I did. I sewed a beautiful lace dress and carefully restored the bisque doll to its original beauty.

This encouraged me to look for similar dolls when I visited estate sales. I found them tossed away amongst plastic toys, discarded without a thought.

These damaged dolls, I restored them. I replaced their wobbly eyes and missing limbs. I dressed them in vintage fabrics as near to the original as possible. I had a small "factory" in the basement, and I sold most of them and also kept a few. I knew some would become more valuable with time. Plus, my daughters admired many of the dolls, and I kept their favorites. I liked the idea of saving something special just for them. I was even asked to restore for museums. It was a good diversion from *the Prince*.

Every week the girls and I hauled a carload of our beautiful, fully restored items to my space at the antique mall. I loved hunting for the antiques and polishing them up. I loved making a sale, and I was proud of my ability to earn money while being with the children.

One weekend at an estate sale on Colorado Boulevard, a man drove up in a long, boxy 1953 Cadillac Reed Ambulance. Big meant safe, and what could be safer than an ambulance? This was no VW Bug that would crumple under me and my kids. So, I asked him, "Would you sell it?"

He smiled and nodded. "$300."

Not only safe, but plenty of room for the girls and me up front. Plus, a ton of space in the back for carting the antiques, meaning no more multiple trips.

I applied stickers of yellow daisies to the ambulance and drove it up and down Colorado Boulevard for years. Everyone recognized it and waved. It was a hoot.

The Yellow Daisy Wonder!

The Yellow Daisy Wonder with Michelle and sister

The doctors where *The Prince* worked thought the ambulance was hysterical. "She can help us," they teased him in front of me about transporting patients.

"I'm just trying to drum up business for you," I teased him, hiding my laughter.

But the sourpuss, *the Prince*, didn't see the humor in it.

I needed humor in my life. Obviously, he didn't enjoy much other than his golf.

I worked hard at my antique business, but you can make only so much money buying and selling glassware on weekends.

I didn't want to scrape by. I wanted more.

One day, when I was setting up my display at the antique mall, standing on a ladder to adjust a sign, I fell and crashed down onto my glassware display table.

Amidst all my shattered treasures, exhausted, I cried. I needed the income from these pieces. I was bringing in decent enough money through the antique business. Some weeks I made good money. Other weeks, however, I barely broke even.

I loved the work, but it was all consuming. Every weekend we went to yard sales, and every weekday the treasures were cleaned. Then we took them to my space on South Broadway.

There must be a better way, I thought. It was a turning point.

My frustration inspired me to think bigger. **I have always believed that when bad things happen, good opportunities will come from it.** I decided I needed a real job, a career, one that would bring in a steady income and allow me to set aside money for a rainy day.

I had thought getting married would give me financial security. It hadn't. *The Prince* was a poor earner, and he had no ambition, no drive. He was a dud of a husband. I was ambitious. At Pan-Am, I had been proud of my independence, and I had liked myself. I wanted to feel that way again.

I looked at all the jobs available to women at the time. The option of flight attendant was gone, and I couldn't be a nurse or a schoolteacher because both required specialized training, which would take too much time away from my time with the children.

What I needed, what I longed for, was a job with flexible hours that would provide me time to care for my children and still bring home a paycheck, all while doing something I would enjoy.

I was intrigued by the real estate profession. In my antiques business, I had spent a great deal of time traipsing through other people's houses at estate sales. This had given me a good sense of homes that would soon be on the housing market. I often thought of ways people could improve their homes. Not only had I learned how to sell and get the best price, I had learned how to make a house more appealing. With just a few simple suggestions to make it more attractive, plus little added touches, I knew I could make a house more presentable.

At estate sales, when scouring through other people's stuff to see what they had collected and decided to discard, I had paid attention to how people decorated their homes. I noticed the floor coverings and the lighting, and I often found myself thinking of ways to improve the house.

Real estate was about knowing what someone wanted and helping them find it.

**I knew my success would be based on this new career, so I worked hard to create financial independence while keeping everything together. I was very focused.**

# 5

# RE/MAX–
# Focusing on Success

## Shattering Barriers

had no clue, however, what was required to get a job in real estate, so I researched, just as I did with the adoption process. I went to open houses and asked a lot of questions. I looked up the licensing requirements: I found out that I was not required to attend school or spend years in training. I only needed to pass a test. My will was strong, but my ability to concentrate was impaired from my accident. I was terrible at passing tests. I had learned how to focus on smaller goals, and tackle them one small step at a time. When I wanted something badly enough, I found a way to get it.

While studying for the real estate exam, I was still solely responsible for running the house, and taking care of the children. I kept clear of *The Prince*, studying for the exam, focusing on what I needed to do for me and the children.

The first time I took the test, I failed. I retained very little of the information I had studied. I did not get frustrated. I'd do better the next time, I decided. *The Prince* laughed at me. He didn't know me. He never had.

I pulled out my study materials and read through them again and again. I had failed the test once but was determined to find a way to pass.

"You can't do this," *The Prince* said and laughed. Out of spite, he took the test himself the next time it was offered, at the same time I did. He passed. I failed, though I scored slightly higher than the first time.

He waved his results in my face. "See. It's easy. You're too stupid."

Incensed, with a fierce defiance and determination, I continued my studies, seeing the test as an obstacle to overcome.

I failed the exam a third time. I still did not give up.

I could have found an easier job, maybe a retail position selling clothes or makeup or perfume. I'd have been good at that. But those jobs offered long hours, low salaries, and I needed to work while still running a household, and taking care of my children.

A career in real estate would give me more than just financial independence. It would give me the freedom to work on my own schedule. I could show houses weekends and evenings. It was the perfect job for me, to take care of myself and my daughters.

I wanted my girls to understand that a woman can be something other than a wife and mother, that women can be strong, successful, and driven. I hoped they would grow up to have good, loving relationships with their partners, something I didn't have. I also hoped they would grow up knowing how to take care of themselves and not to rely on a man for everything. I had to show them it was possible. Before I took the exam for the fourth time, the test administrator pulled me aside.

"This real estate school enjoys a high success rate. Most people who take the exam pass it; 99 percent pass it on their first try. People rarely take the exam twice."

"I will pass it," I said. "It's just going to take me a little more time."

"You're bringing down the average," he said.

"There are no rules about how many times I can take the exam, I replied. "Please reconsider taking the test again," he continued.

"You underestimate me," I replied.

On the fourth time, I failed the test again—even though my score was higher than before. I was getting closer.

I no longer doubted that I would pass the test.

It was the same every time, but it was long. I needed to memorize it. I knew I could do it. I only had to score 75 percent to pass the exam.

No one understood why passing this exam was important to me. At that time, I was not prepared to leave my marriage, though somewhere in the back of my mind I knew I couldn't stay with *The Prince* much longer.

I needed to know I could make it on my own, and I felt there was only one path forward for me. I had to pass the real estate exam.

On my fifth try, I passed. The man who had told me I was destroying his organization's success rate congratulated me.

"I didn't think you would do it," he said. "I knew I would," I replied.

**It's hard to beat someone who never gives up.**

With my license in hand, I went to find a job. It wasn't easy. Only a handful of women were working in real estate. It was a man's world.

I went to agency after agency: "We already have a woman …. We are not hiring now, but we need someone to answer the phones and set up appointments."

I had worked too hard to be a receptionist.

I finally got a desk at a small company, but they did not train me on the basic skills of a real estate agent. When I did manage to bring in a listing on my own, they charged me 50 percent of my commission, and they tried to undercut me by sending a male agent to handle the showings. It was infuriating. But I kept my head down and I worked hard.

Soon, I heard about a new agency setting up in Denver. It wasn't structured in the old way. Instead, this agency would let me set up my own office and handle my own listings. I could set my own commissions and hours. They didn't care that I was female. If I worked hard and brought in business, that was the goal.

RE/MAX was a bold idea, giving the agent, not the broker, responsibility for his or her own success.

"We don't provide coffee, pencils or even a desk," the founder, Dave Liniger told me. "You're on your own. You pay us a small fee, but you keep 100 percent of your commissions. Just sell out of the back of your car." I promptly set up office in the back of my car.

RE/MAX was the perfect fit. I had so much fun. I always figured it out. I took risks and prided myself on my maverick spirit. I had to be clever, and I went to great lengths to make a sale, and give my clients more than they expected.

There was a house under court order to be sold in a divorce decree in the exclusive Denver Country Club neighborhood. The husband still lived in the house and refused to let anyone show it, making it impossible to sell.

Only certain agents sold in the Country Club area, and none were Jewish or women. However, I knew the man's wife. So, I hatched a plan.

I wrote up a contract and called the wife "I have a buyer," I said.

She put me in contact with her lawyer, and through a court order, we had one hour to view the house.

The court order didn't state how many people could be in the house during the hour. So, I invited every major agent to view the house, with their clients.

I walked through the crowd of male agents and their clients who were waiting on the lawn. One agent looked me up and down. "This is the Club area, my dear. You obviously don't belong here. Go sell in Hilltop."

I hid my fear. "You have one hour to get your client in." Accessing all my courage, I walked right up to the door and knocked. I didn't let my fear of what could happen stop me.

A federal marshal answered and looked at the crowd in shock. "Who are all these people?"

I looked him in the eye. "We have an hour to view the house.

These are wealthy people, and they have many advisors." In disbelief, he stepped aside.

Within thirty minutes, I held a check that would hold the house and an agreement with an agent to write a contract. "Be sure to put in a six percent commission," I told him.

He smiled. "You're new. It's seven percent."

My reputation was cemented as someone who will do what is needed to sell a house.

When the houses were not selling in Denver, and listings would often last for a year, I figured out a way to help the sellers (whose homes were vacant), and victims of domestic violence at the same time. I would set up these women (who often had great furniture) in the vacant homes rent-free, helping them get back on their feet. Many times they had children that benefitted as well. The owner of the vacant home benefitted because their house was now staged, which helped it to sell, and their insurance became considerably more affordable since insurance companies raise premiums drastically on vacant homes. It was a win-win for both parties.

RE/MAX's reputation grew quickly as well. Soon, many of the best agents in town were clamoring to work there. The first offices were in the Denver Tech Center, but I still worked out of the back of my car. I had someplace to be every day.

I was in business!

RE/MAX provided the most unique value to the agents. Their signs displayed the agent's name in large letters and the agents got to advertise themselves at the same time as the RE/MAX agency. We kept 100% of our commission and did not have to split it. We just had to pay a reasonable desk fee. It encouraged individual responsibility to secure your own listings and create buyers instead of depending on an agency to give you clients.

Every realtor competed to get brokers to tour their listings. That agent brought the food and set up. Getting brokers to show up to view listings and creating a buzz was the goal. For my Broker Open House, I hired a woman who usually worked at bachelor parties to manage my Wednesday morning tour. She sat in the middle of the bed in the master bedroom, completely naked, reading a magazine. One realtor walked out speechless. Another struck up a conversation with her. After that, everyone came to my Broker Open Houses—a naked woman was never needed again!

We competed to have the best wine and food, so brokers would look at our houses during lunch. Although our invitations read like a gourmet restaurant, I served the opposite. I offered an "array of Nabisco crackers and saltines, served with vintage Kool-Aid and classic Velveeta cheese." My outlandish humor and surprises made my open houses fun.

Once, when I had no food prepared, I cleaned out the freezer at home, the dregs of my own "burnt offerings." I drizzled "gourmet sauce" over my freezer-burned food. It was awful but we weren't there to eat. I didn't think anyone would even notice. Then a coworker called from the ER.

"What did you feed us!" he said in a panic.

I hung up on him, afraid I had poisoned my colleagues. He called back. "April Fools!" It was the first time anyone had fooled me on April Fool's Day. It was an office joke. With my penchant for my own April Fool's gags, I fit right in at RE/MAX.

Quite a few agents began asking me for advice about marketing. Some didn't talk to me, but just copied everything I did: the calendars, the park benches, the brochures, my funny advertising. I was always flattered, never offended, when they copied my ideas. I always believed the saying that imitation is the best form of flattery.

An agent in our office had no sense of humor, and was not approachable. He was great with paperwork and contracts, but he had no clue about marketing. I proposed a trade. I would handle his marketing if he drew up my contracts. At first, he balked. But he could see that I was getting more listings and that my clients liked me. He agreed, and we worked that way for years. **It is always to your advantage to acknowledge your weaknesses, and delegate, so you are able to create other opportunities. It also allows you to concentrate on your strengths, and not quit because of these weaknesses.**

We do better when we surround ourselves with people who complement us. Through all these experiences, I had learned never to take "no" for an answer. I also tried to save money whenever possible, shopping at thrift stores and garage sales. **You get what you focus on, and I focused on being successful and financially independent and was always working to achieve that goal.**

I realized as an agent that I was different. I was unafraid, and a risk taker. I had a single-minded determination to succeed.

My childhood was good training for my new career in real estate. I knew how to put my best face forward, smile, and be empathetic. I had been putting on a happy face since I was a young child.

RE/MAX was a barebones operation, and I was only the second female agent hired at that time. Yet they treated me as an equal. It was hard work that mattered most to them, not gender.

In the beginning, I worked out of my car. Eventually, I settled into an office. As the offices didn't come equipped with a desk, file cabinet, or landline telephone—mobiles were a thing of the future—I had to bring in everything. Fortunately, my years of antique hunting made finding furniture a snap.

In the office, we agents did our own thing. And we had fun!

We worked hard and laughed a lot. It was refreshing to spend my days there, which was a stark departure from my life with *The Prince.*

I also had fun with clients, but usually because I sometimes forgot which role I was in, professional real estate agent or mother.

Once at a lunch meeting with a top executive client, I reached across the table and began to cut his steak into small pieces. I was so used to doing it for my kids, I didn't even think about it.

He looked at me oddly. "What the hell are you doing?"

As I tried to explain, we both started laughing. There were many moments when my maternal instincts overtook my business sense. Fortunately, most people have a good sense of humor about such things.

From the beginning of my real estate career, I had to work harder than the other agents. Writing contracts made me nervous, and I made many mistakes.

Today, an agent pulls a file from the city or brings in an appraiser. When I started, we measured the houses on our own, and I'm not a math whiz.

Once, when I set the square footage incorrectly for a listing, I was told I should get a lawyer because they were going to dispute it. This could have turned into a big ordeal, but I knew all I had to do was tell the truth and admit I had screwed up. That's not an easy thing to do, but it's almost always the right thing to do.

I didn't get a lawyer and I didn't fight the dispute. <u>I took responsibility for my mistake</u> and asked how much it would cost to make things right. I paid the money they asked for without arguing.

This cost me my entire commission and then some. It really set me back, while I was just getting started in the business, but I learned my lesson: I couldn't do everything myself. Accepting that my brain wasn't wired for calculating numbers, I asked for help and never again measured a home myself. I paid an expert.

After this, I worked with other people to double- and triple- check my work. I learned to always **"hire my weakness."** I didn't want any more calls from lawyers and I definitely couldn't afford to lose another commission. Living in terror of closing on a house with a bad contract, I learned to be wary with parts of the business.

In other ways, I excelled. I learned that I had a knack for marketing. In the early years, I took photos of the houses in my neighborhood and turned them into calendars of each specific home. I delivered these to the homeowners during the winter holidays. It was a ton of work. There were no digital cameras then, and there was no way to see if I had taken a good photo until the film was developed.

With my camera, I took over 3,000 photos every year and learned a lot about lighting. In the fall, I chose the best shot of each house and pasted them all into the calendars, which I then wrapped in cellophane and personally delivered to the homeowners. I put my name and contact information on the front of the calendars so when people decided to put their homes on the market, they would think of me first. Spencer Mamba, who owned MotoPhoto, suffered the consequences of my photography- I am still dear friends with him today, he is now a RE/MAX agent, and has always been a kind supporter.

The calendars were great advertising because they had a long shelf life. People kept them because they were pictures of their own homes. Years later, their children would call me and tell me they had those calendars, that their parents had cherished them. Soon, I was handling their listings as well. Even in the winter, when other realtors advised to wait until spring, I already had boxes of pictures from the spring to use.

Another idea was to hand potential sellers a matchbook, with the saying: "Call Denice Reich to sell your house ... because if she can't, you might as well burn it down." In small print: "For marketing purposes only, not for burning down your home." This gave people a great laugh.

Matchbook advertisement

When Andrew was five, he helped me deliver the calendars and the homeowners remarked how cute he was.

I also sent humorous brochures to my neighborhood.

When other agents called places "charming" or "rustic," I told people straight out they could get a good deal in a good neighborhood if they were willing to overlook some flaws.

One house had a bathroom next to the kitchen and, instead of a toilet, had a bidet. In the brochure, I said, "Start your day with coffee and a bidet."

I typed and pasted everything up by hand and ran copies on a Xerox machine at the office. There were no computers to do it for me. The brochures weren't fancy, but they were memorable, with clip art that made people smile and kept me in the forefront of their minds.

One of my first listings was the iconic Richtofen Castle in the Montclair neighborhood. The stone castle had quite a storied history and was considered a white elephant. Built in the 1880s by Walter von Richtofen, uncle of the World War I pilot known as the Red Baron, the castle was perhaps best known as the site of the 1911 murder of Charles Patterson by his wife, Gertrude.

She was often referred to as "the most beautiful woman in the world." Her husband had a jealous streak and during a fight, she shot him. Witnesses at the trial claimed she had secured a "not guilty" verdict by showing her ankles in court.

The thirty-five room castle was rumored to be haunted—a good selling point for tourists but not great for homebuyers. No matter what, I was determined to make a good sale. The castle was huge, old, and rundown.

Former owners had neglected entire wings of the castle. Some had installed tacky modern embellishments that diminished the grandeur of the place. No one wanted to buy the monstrosity. That was until I got my hands on it and recorded the second highest sale for a "mansion" in Denver at the time.

I had very little money to market the castle. So, I called a reporter from United Press International and told him there was a real castle for sale in the West. He published the story in numerous newspapers across the U.S. and I met wealthy prospective buyers at the airport.

Still, the castle wasn't selling. It needed so much work. I convinced the Denver Symphony Guild to use the castle as their show home. They hired designers who pulled down the old wallpaper, brought in new rugs and trendy furniture. Unfortunately, they also took out a wall and left piles of plaster on the second floor.

I had Michelle's fifth birthday party at the castle and gave prizes to the girls who could throw the most lathe and plaster out the windows. The girls had a ton of fun, although their mothers were appalled at how filthy they were when they picked them up.

# Lady of Richtofen

*by Scott Awbrey*

"The Richtofen Castle is an urban villa in Central Denver. Located in the historic neighborhood of Montclair, it is secluded on one acre of land. You enter the Castle through lovely old wrought iron gates. A circular drive and large old trees give you a feeling of living in a time of serene quality.

"Total privacy dominates the theme of the Castle. It has 21 beautifully proportioned rooms done in oak and pecan. The six fireplaces — leaded glass windows — secret panels — exquisite entrance are only a few highlights that add to the character of this English Manor Home. It is a family home of warmth and comfort, a masterpiece of quality."

So begins the script of the listing information brochure professionally designed and written with quality illustrations and photographs to aid a REALTOR in selling a half-million-dollar castle.

But the sale of the Richtofen Castle was not nearly as smooth and polished as the impression left by the brochure. Denice Reich of RE/MAX East, Inc. in Denver undertook the project of listing the "white elephant" more than three years ago, and she quickly learned selling the castle was no easy task.

Professionalism — the key word

Article about Richtofen Castle Listing

My drive to succeed did lead me to take on some projects I should have avoided. An attorney asked me to list a house on 13th and Columbine, which had been condemned. Home to a cat hoarder, there had been 135 cats in the home and five had died behind the refrigerator, leaving a stench. I met the health department representative there. After touring the house, he went in the backyard and vomited. I had lost my sense of smell in my car crash at sixteen, so I wasn't bothered at all.

I decided to have an estate sale to empty the house before readying it for sale. I moved the furniture and found gorgeous vintage clothes that I took to the cleaners. The attendant stopped me at the door and said, "Don't even think of coming inside. The smell will permeate the store and I'll never get rid of it."

Taking the clothes back, I began the estate sale anyway.

Everything looked good enough. I thought it would be fine after a bit of airing out, but many people wouldn't come inside. They came to the front door and turned green.

I was surprised when the sale was a complete flop because there were so many lovely things. After two other realtors threw up trying to tour the house, I ended up selling to an investor for pennies on the dollar. The investor completely removed the saturated wood floors, plaster, and studs because the urine had permeated the entire house.

Some of my endeavors were more successful than others. I listed the house of a friend's mother, who was dying of cancer.

She wanted to move to a condo so her husband would be okay after she was gone. They had paid off their loan twenty years prior but, when we went to the bank, the sale wasn't recorded, and the bank refused to correct the mistake. The bank acknowledged they didn't owe on the house but wanted them to post a "lost instruments bond," a document that had to be posted in the newspaper.

I spent a day at the bank going back and forth. Finally, I took the stamp used for parking, stamped the Farber's paperwork, and wrote "Paid in full." I remembered what my father taught me: **When you want something done, find your own solutions.**

I had one (of several clients) who had just moved to Denver after graduating from an Ivy League university. He was extremely worried with letting me know "how important he was." He told me that he would get another realtor if I did not agree to all his requests. He insisted I find him houses that were being foreclosed on, and had not yet been listed. By chance I found one in the Observatory Park neighborhood of Denver, and called the bank to make an appointment to show to my client. It was only two years old. When I told him they were not able to give me an appointment for six weeks, his reply was, "you get me into that house sooner." I drove by, and noticed the front door was gone (a very large front door). I called him and told him we could just walk in, as the house should not be occupied, and the front door was missing. He met me at the house with his wife and two young daughters. The interior of the house was in total disarray. All the appliances were missing, most kitchen cabinets were gone, many of the bathroom fixtures were also missing, and the garage had suffered fire damage on one side – with no garage door. We proceeded upstairs, and I was shocked at the expensive artwork and clothing that remained.

The house itself was filthy. I kept calling out in each room to make sure it was unoccupied – it was vacant. We proceeded to the basement, my client beat me to the doors, and pushed them open. Inside, one of the foreclosed owners was having sex with a man. It shocked the client, but he still made an offer on the home. I spent an entire day getting him quotes on new appliances, carpet, painting, etc. His offer was quite low, and the bank accepted another contract six months later.

Then I bought a house with my own money, thinking I would rent it out. It was a small lot in the Cherry Creek neighborhood at 450 St. Paul for only $59,000 but on one of the best blocks.

It made sense to add a bathroom in the basement. I didn't have the money to hire a plumber and contractor, but I knew I had to connect the basement sewer line to the city sewer tap, if I could just find it.

The girls and I dug along the sewer line starting in the outside back of the house and continuing across the backyard. We dug every Saturday and Sunday, a ten-foot deep trench that extended from the house to the alley. It took months, but we reached the sewer tap! It was a huge project, but I'd done a ton of home repair myself over the years.

Unfortunately, someone reported us to the city, and the city inspector showed up. He insisted we get out of the trench and stop digging. "Do you know how dangerous this is? It could collapse, and it's illegal that you're trying to connect to the city sewer."

He then just shook his head. "I'll forget I ever saw it, but you must call a plumber immediately."

I think he couldn't believe I had tried to tackle such a project on my own. I occasionally ran into him over the years. He was always respectful and kind, and never said a word. I was very lucky.

Then I noticed we had a dead tree in the backyard. The girls and I sawed through it a little at a time over many days. We got it down, but it knocked off the corner of our garage and took out some electrical lines. The whole block lost electricity. But we no longer had a dead tree in the yard!

Not to be left out, the upstairs bathroom in my home needed new tile, so I got to work on it myself. The old tile was set in concrete and it was a chore to chip it out a bit at a time. I figured if I removed the joists, I could remove the concrete slabs completely. I finished the job and was pleased with myself, until later that week. I was sitting at the kitchen table and noticed some cracks in the ceiling. Moments later, the bathtub came crashing through and landed in the middle of the kitchen. I had to have the bathroom floor redone and steel beams installed to fix the support lost when I had removed the joists. I was always learning, and sometimes my drive got me into trouble.

I also installed a new basement bathroom in another house where, thankfully, the sewer line was already connected. I did the installation myself, I was so full of energy, but I neglected to get the proper permits.

When the city assessor was scheduled to come by to assess the main floor, I was afraid he would turn me in for installing the new bathroom. I didn't want my shoddy work discovered, so I paid a homeless man twenty dollars to stay in the basement and bark whenever the inspectors came by. It was a narrow escape. I finally learned that it wasn't always a good idea to tackle every project on my own, that sometimes I needed to ask for help and pay an expert.

One home I listed on 6th Ave. had 2 sewer lines to a single home - one was blocked, and the sewer company technician went into the basement to try and clear the blocked one, and told the technician outside to "turn on the jets" Not only was he covered in his mistake, but the entire room was also a stinking mess. Another sewer story was when a 12 ft sewer lid covered the back patio of a house. I questioned the seller who just had purchased the home and was immediately putting it back on the market as to why it was there. He stated he had no idea. I then called Denver Wastewater Management since their name was on the lid. They sent a letter stating that the entire sewer system made a "turn underneath that home, and that (in fact) the house had not been built in the 1940s on a valid permit. If anything happened causing the sewer line needing to be repaired, the house would have to be destroyed. He (the new owner) responded, "Denice, just between "us girls", we don't need to disclose that, do we") I told him we did. He wanted to know what my solution was - I told him to buy yellow and brown carpet and keep it as a rental.

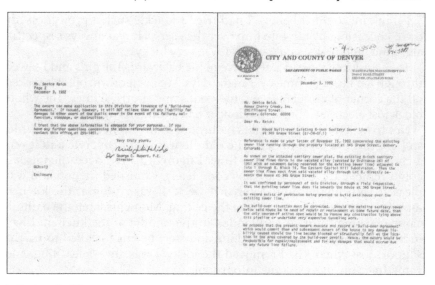

Letter from the City

One time a professor of law at a major university had large, heavy drapes from wall to wall that overpowered the room. The house was not selling, and I told him that the drapes had to go, and I would also paint his pink walls. He was resistant. When I stated that I would pay for the removal of the drapes, and the painting of the walls, he agreed. To my astonishment, after the drapes were removed a giant crack an inch wide was revealed across the entire room. I let him know that had to be fixed and disclosed. After that, the property sold.

Another client, a renowned psychiatrist, built a large addition without any foundation or permits. When it started to separate from the main structure, he put throw rugs with dirt underneath to hide what was happening and insisted on getting a sales price for his home that was way over the highest home listed at that time. The listing went through 4 realtors and sold years later, with many disclosures.

One time, my real estate partner at the time, Stephanie, and myself went on a listing, and the seller called us and said he was at "An undisclosed location, but to put his house on the market, and sell everything in it." After he signed the listing, we told him we would conduct an estate sale for him there. It was on a busy street, we put all the contents together, and it seemed like it would be an easy task, as there was no basement, just a lot of items. We then discovered an attic above the garage, and I said to Stephanie, "let's pull the attic stairs down, and see if there is anything up there." We found a plethora of sex related items, and as we were throwing them down the opening, there was a lot of shock and awe. We had a very unusual and successful sale, almost everything sold. I did have a problem selling the family photographs and held those for him. When I called him, he said he did not want them. The same afternoon, a middle-aged woman came to the house and asked where the owner was, and if there were any family pictures. She then stated she was a relative, and just wanted the family photos - because her husband was his son and had committed suicide. I was thrilled to give them to her.

corn maze joke

One of our favorite clients was a man who taught us about foreclosures. He took us under his wing. We had met him at the foreclosure auctions, and to "educate" us, he would send us "dumb blonde jokes."

On Halloween, he sent us a corn maze for "dumb blondes" - it was one stalk of corn. So I brought (to his Christmas party), a trash can lid that I had embedded a pair of men's shoes in cement to - as he liked to refer to himself as "The Godfather of Foreclosures."

My very favorite client, who taught me so much, was Terry Combs. When we received a contract on his home (I was the listing agent), he told me that he knew the buyer's dad. He then said, "I will just go ahead and put the whole deal together." Of course the other agent balked at the thought of getting a buyer and seller together. She insisted she go with the buyer to Terry's house, because in real estate 101, you never get a buyer and seller together. Terry sat the agent down in the far end of the house, and met with the buyer in his study. I was not present, and the buyer's agent was not invited to the meeting he had with the buyer in the study. He then called me, and said, "I just put the whole deal together, so I want a discount on my commission." I obliged - I had and still have, nothing but respect for him. I learned from that experience, to always keep the deal together - don't just blindly follow arbitrary "rules." On the last house I sold for him, the buyer was so afraid that he would lose money on the house, that he kept insisting that, "if in 2 years I want to sell the house I am afraid I will end up losing money, so I wrote a low offer." Again, Terry met with the buyer, and told him, "I will buy the house back in 2 years for what you paid for it." The buyer said, "What if I don't want to sell?" Terry said, "That's irrelevant, I am solving your immediate worry." The buyer decided instead of that, to offer full price for the house. It was a brilliant strategy. I was, and am, in awe of his sales talent.

Another interesting sale was when there were ten houses built in the 1980's in a circle. They were all friends and wanted main floor ranches. Of course, in later years, a fight between the owners ensued. The fight started because the grandchildren of one of the original owners was "too noisy" when they used the community pool. It was a very tough listing. I finally had someone interested in the property, the client was a minority, and I brought him over to view on a Sunday afternoon, when all the other owners were sitting outside by the pool. The other nine owners had "Right of First Refusal" to any buyer. After my client went to view the property, they exercised that right, and purchased the property together. From that moment on, the seller of the home always referred to me as, "Mrs. Moses", because he thought I walked on water.

I once listed a house on 6$^{th}$ Ave. that had to be sold because of a divorce. The new buyer gave her a full price offer, but he wanted the playground equipment she had excluded. She directed me to give him a credit of $12,000 but would not let him retain the playground equipment. The contract fell because she would not budge. The market then went south. After going through 3 additional realtors, she finally called me to relist the house. It sold for $150,000 less than the original contract from three years previous. The children were older, and the playground equipment stayed with the sale. Years later I ran into the new buyer, he said he had just given the playground equipment away. I also had a similar story with a refrigerator. I learned from this that when a buyer and seller argue over an irrelevant item, it's best for me to just purchase the item if I can and keep the deal together. The owner of the refrigerator said, "I will not let that son of a bitch have that refrigerator" When his house sold for less a year later, and the movers were moving the refrigerator out, I said "It certainly does not look like a $50,000 refrigerator."

Wrecking ball from demolition protest

One time an historic house was going to be demolished. I felt fed up with the city for allowing this, and letting developers replace with box house. I went with a few other protesters, climbed up the wrecking machine, and removed the wrecking ball. Although that only delayed the demolition by a day, I keep that wrecking ball in my garden to remind me of all the beautiful historic houses that no longer exist in Denver.

I represented a very finan-cially strong couple who wanted to purchase a house. They would bid on houses as soon as they were available on the market, and would offer good prices, contingent upon the inspection. When the inspection was about to expire, they would ask for an extension. Then they would cancel the contract based on the inspection contingencies. Usually right at midnight, before the contingency expired. After they had done this to the third property they wrote a contract on, (which happened to be my listing), I felt so bad for the 80 year old sellers, because they were packed and ready to move to Arizona. They were supposed to close in 3 days before the contract was cancelled. We were all shocked. They always assured me they would close. On the fourth house, they convinced me again that they were absolutely going through with the deal. I was wary of their intentions to actually close, so had a back-up buyer (since this was also my listing), and the seller's wife was dying of cancer, and the house had to sell. Of course, they backed out in the end. I finally figured out that their misuse of power was actually a game they enjoyed playing. They had no understanding, or didn't care if they did, of what they put the seller's through – it was all about them, their power, and their lack of empathy. I then wrote them (when they cancelled the last deal), that I was shocked they could have had three children because he pulled out of every deal. Even after I sent that letter, they asked me to list their house when they wanted to sell.

You also had to be careful at listings. I had a woman who always came to my open houses and would ask if she could use the rest room. I thought it was odd, and discovered she was an addict who would steal medicine out of the client's bathrooms.

Another of my favorite stories had to do with a lender. She actually sent me an email (after I had sent a death certificate for the wife of the man selling), to "Please have the deceased sign all the documents."

There were also very interesting, decorated homes for sale. There once was a 1930s English Tudor home that had 3 family rooms, and 3 floor to ceiling safes. One of the family rooms contained a large aquarium surrounded by a bar with 20 barstools. I questioned the seller, "Why the safes and the aquarium?" He said it had aways been that way since he purchased the property 30 years previously. I had a buyer, who purchased the home "As-Is", he called me after the closing and said, "I touched a mirror in the master bedroom, and it opened an entire filing cabinet." So amazing. It held all the files of prominent Denver society. This was the place where all the prominent citizens of Denver gambled in the 30s, 40s, and 50s. He also showed me the laundry chute, which was filled with telephone lines that went throughout the entire house.

One of my early real estate clients was a doctor. His lovely old two-story house had great street appeal. The inside was something else; it was simply awful. It hadn't been touched since it was built in the 1930s. The flowered wallpaper and indoor/outdoor carpet were smelly and covered in years of dog hair. The avocado green kitchen appliances and cabinets had been purchased in the 1950s. I knew I would have to make some changes in order to sell the house. Asking a seller to change the home wasn't done in the 1970s, nor was staging. I didn't want to offend the doctor, so I waited until he went to Santa Fe, New Mexico, on vacation. While he was gone, I steamed off the wallpaper, painted, pulled up carpet, put $1,600 into refinishing the hardwood, and removed the heavy dark drapes. I had a moving service remove the furniture and put it in storage, replacing it with almost all the furniture from my own house. I was afraid I wouldn't sell the house, so I slept there and made it available for showings morning, noon, and night. I quickly received a contract on the house and mailed it express to the doctor in Santa Fe. He mailed it back immediately, happy to have sold his house. He already had accepted a job out of state.

Another client called in desperation when his house wouldn't sell. I redid the yard and made small improvements. In the spring, his home sold for $50,000 over his previous listing.

Buyers often lack vision and need to see a house at its best. A fresh paint job or new carpet can make the difference, as well as rearranging furniture. Prospective homebuyers need to be able to imagine living there as if it's their own home. Real estate was exciting – every day was different. The clients, the houses – they all presented life's happenings. You were a participant in the outcomes. Sometimes it was heartbreaking, sometimes it was the most joyful of events.

**There is always a solution to every problem, in real estate and in life, and I felt grateful to have this career.**

In the 1970s, most agents showed houses without much embellishment. Thanks to my experience with the Richtofen Castle, I knew that most homes benefit from a makeover. My innovative ideas gave me an advantage in the market. My listings stood out, and they sold.

*The Prince* would often come home and find the sofa missing. Visitors at our house would ask if we had been robbed. *The Prince* took his frustration out on me, but soon I was making real money and we needed the income.

In those early days, I did a lot of the work myself. Today, there are entire companies devoted to "staging" houses. It's an art. When I first started doing it, I worked on instinct. No one else in Denver was "staging" listings. The word … the strategy … the profession didn't exist then. I figured it out on my own. It set me apart. **My business model was, always give more than expected.**

# 6

# Accepting the Unacceptable

Surrogacy to Poisoning of Son

M y inner voice was growing stronger. Emerging was a woman fighting to trust her own mind. It did not happen overnight.

Many days I still faced the world with blinders. It's not easy to reverse a lifetime of behaviors. Valuing my own ideas and opinions was growing stronger.

At work, I was confident, successful, and respected. My days were filled with my real estate career, my children's school and after school activities, and running the household.

I loved being a mother.

I wasn't thinking about adoption this time, but surrogacy.

Before we had adopted Kay, I had researched other possibilities. Surrogacy, still in its infancy, struck me as promising.

I purchased an advertisement in a college newspaper, offering to pay the tuition of a healthy young woman who would carry a baby for me. It seemed like a great idea.

The call I got wasn't from a student but a single young mother. She had a seven-year-old daughter and she was looking for innovative ways to make money.

"I love being pregnant," she said. "I would be happy to do it again."

I liked her immediately. She was funny, warm and intelligent.

We agreed to meet for lunch. I brought *The Prince* along, which was a terrible mistake. At the time, no one would serve as a surrogate without meeting both parents, to assure that both wanted the baby.

*The Prince* did not support my desire for a baby. Even though he came that day, he tried to sabotage the deal.

The possible surrogate (Claudia), however, was everything I had hoped she would be, and we hit it off. I felt like we were old friends. I knew I could trust her. We had so much in common. She was also a real estate agent. So, we agreed on a fee.

Surrogacy was like the Wild West then. There weren't many rules. When I talked to a lawyer, he said, "You're nuts. Don't do it."

"You could be arrested for trafficking children."

Against my better judgment, Claudia and I decided it was too risky. I was deeply disappointed.

By 1984, Maura was in college, Michelle was nearly fourteen, and Kay had just turned ten. I was still determined to have another child. I couldn't go through the pain of private adoption again. I couldn't stand in the parking lot of a hospital hoping a woman would surrender her baby to me.

So, I poured my energies into my real estate work, taking on more listings and putting in longer and longer hours.

Three years later, while working on a listing for a Denver gynecologist, I noticed a stack of files on his kitchen counter labeled "Surrogates."

"I'm hoping to start a surrogacy program in Denver," he said when I asked about the files.

He'd spent the past year interviewing potential surrogates and assessing their fitness, psychologically and physically. He had seventeen good candidates, but he hadn't yet found the other side of the equation: the couples who wanted to give birth using a surrogate.

I told him of my interest and said, "That's exactly what I want."

He allowed me to flip through his files to see if any of the profiles were a good fit.

The files didn't contain identifying information. The women were defined only by physical details, such as race, hair color, and general health, or cultural details such as religion and education. The surrogates were supposed to be completely anonymous, to circumvent pitfalls that might arise between a surrogate and the woman whose child she carried.

As I flipped through the files, one stood out. The description of the woman was very familiar. I was positive it was Claudia. I couldn't believe my luck. What were the odds. It had been three years and she was still interested in being a surrogate?

Although the prevailing advice at the time was that the surrogate should remain anonymous, I believed we could work together.

I found Claudia's number and called her. We both regretted that we had taken the lawyer's advice and abandoned our plans before.

"When are you ovulating?" I asked her.

"Saturday," she replied.

Now where am I going to find some sperm? I wondered.

I had only a few days to find donor sperm. I didn't want *The Prince* involved.

That weekend I had a listing appointment with a couple in Denver. The husband seemed smart and even-tempered. I thought it couldn't hurt to ask.

I explained my situation to them.

They were appalled.

When I'm pursuing something, I am single-minded and intense. All I could see was the outcome: a baby. Sometimes not stopping until I get what I want is my best asset, like when I was determined to pass my real estate exam or be accepted for the PanAm job. Sometimes it was also my worst asset, like asking a stranger for sperm. I realized it might not be easy. I couldn't just ask any man for his sperm.

Claudia's gynecologist informed me that the University of Colorado, on the forefront of the cryogenics movement, ran a sperm bank. All I had to do was purchase a sample.

I flipped through the files of anonymous men, on age, race, religion, and medical history. I wanted someone tall and intelligent, with a good, healthy background.

I wanted my baby to have every possible advantage, and Claudia had a great sense of humor, a good personality, and she was attractive and athletic.

I found a man who fit the bill and called Claudia. "We're in business!"

On the day of the insemination, I took a taxi to the sperm bank and picked up the sample. It was a cold day. On the way to the doctor's office for the procedure, I held the container in my hands to keep it warm.

In the 1980's, artificial insemination was used primarily to assist married couples with fertility problems. It often failed or required multiple procedures, and no one talked about it openly. It usually required several rounds for a woman to become pregnant.

We were lucky. Shortly after the first procedure, Claudia called me. "We're pregnant!"

We'd devised our own surrogacy arrangement with nothing but a handshake. Over the next nine months, we became close. On weekends, she came over to my house and brought her daughter. Our girls played together while Claudia and I baked bread and talked. It was a magical time. I got to watch her belly grow with my baby. I felt the baby kick. It was wonderful.

Claudia glowed and seemed to have more energy as the pregnancy progressed. It was an easy, stress-free time. *The Prince* cleared out of the house every weekend for golf. Claudia, the girls and I spent the hours together, laughing, eating and playing games.

Over Christmas break, *The Prince* took our girls to a resort in Manzanillo, Mexico, for our annual two-week vacation. I did not go, since Claudia was due to give birth any day, and I did not want to miss the birth.

Sure enough, she called while they were on vacation., "I'm in labor!"

I met her at Rose Medical Center in Denver, and stayed with her throughout the birth, marveling at how easy it was.

Soon I was holding a beautiful baby boy in my arms: Andrew. He was healthy, pink, and happy from day one.

As planned, Claudia and I filed the papers for stepparent adoption, listing *The Prince* as the father, the only way I was allowed to legally adopt.

All the horror stories and warnings about surrogacy did not happen. It was one of the easiest things I had ever done and certainly the most valuable. All the lawyers who warned against entering into surrogacy agreements, doctors who warned it might not work, experts who said the mother and surrogate should never meet, they were all wrong in my case.

I had sensed this years earlier when I first met Claudia.

I knew it would work for us.

My only regret was that Claudia and I didn't do it sooner.

That year became a tipping point for me— I resolved to start trusting my instincts. I had accepted other people's opinions, criticisms, warnings, and advice over my own for my entire life. I'd spent so much of my life striving to be someone else's idea of perfect, that I hardly knew how to be myself.

Holding my infant son in my arms helped me to understand how important it was for me to be authentic in all areas of my life. I had been too willing to bend to other people's expectations. Since childhood, I had been told to act and look a certain way, and what to expect and want from life. I had lived with blinders on and marched to their drums. No more, that stopped now.

People always questioned why I wanted children with such a successful career. **I always knew that trophies were put on a shelf, and easily forgotten, while children, and the memories of your time together are part of your life forever.**

*The Prince* and the girls returned from the holiday, and I introduced them to Andrew. The girls doted on him.

The first months with Andrew were some of the best of my life. It was winter, a slow time for the real estate market, so I made the most of it. I would be working long hours soon enough when spring arrived, historically when the majority of homes were listed.

I was forty-three now, and was earning a good living, there was no reason for me to try and do everything myself. Maura was grown. Michelle was a teenager, helping around the house when I asked, but busy with school and her own friends. Kay, at ten, still needed my attention.

Andrew was an infant. I realized that I needed a nanny. A live-in nanny would give Andrew consistency and security. She could help with meals and the morning routine and be home with Kay and Michelle after school.

I researched the nanny agencies I could find and settled on one of the best rated programs in the country. They had been written up in LIFE magazine and were highly recommended. I went to their Denver branch. They sent me Carolyn. She was about my age and had a son in college. She came with glowing recommendation letters, including one from the governor of Colorado for her political volunteering. I hired her, and she moved into our basement.

The housing market that spring, in the mid-1980's real estate boom, was busier than ever. It seemed everyone wanted to buy. I maintained my spot as one of the top realtors in Denver, but it kept me busy.

Andrew seemed happy and healthy. Even in his first months, I could tell he was smart. He was always curious and lively, and very cuddly.

Carolyn was always with us, and we treated her as a member of the family. Michelle bonded with her. She joined our family in Aspen for our annual summer vacation. It was a relief to have her help.

Because we had Carolyn, when I spent time with my children, I could relax and enjoy their company rather than constantly managing the household. I felt like I finally had balance in my life.

Then in late May, Carolyn's personality changed. She became hostile and angry. It frightened me enough that I started taking Andrew with me to work every day. I called the agency and expressed my concerns. "I need someone else." "You're probably just tired," the agency responded.

I believed them—because I still doubted myself, yet I couldn't shake the feeling that something was wrong. I kept Andrew with me most of the time and used Carolyn as a helper, mainly preparing meals and helping me run the household. I made a point not to leave her alone with him more than necessary.

Labor Day weekend 1985, we invited friends over for a barbecue. The house overflowed with guests. It was a beautiful, clear, warm night. Michelle and Kay were headed back to school the following week. Andrew was nine months old. He was teething, cranky, and quick to cry.

After the party ended, I was exhausted. Most nights, I spent time cuddling with Andrew, but that night I was more tired than usual. Carolyn was a great help during the party, welcoming and seeing our guests. I thought perhaps I had misjudged her. Maybe the agency was right—it was just my exhaustion. I asked her to take care of Andrew. He was crying when I went to bed. Soon his cries quieted down.

I woke to Carolyn's panicked screams at three a.m. My heart racing, I flew down the stairs. She was holding Andrew and crying. "The baby is dead! He's not breathing!"

I took him from her into my arms. He was breathing, but it was shallow and weak, and he felt strangely limp. "Wake up! Wake up!" I begged. *The Prince* came in and took a quick look. "He's fine. Don't be such a drama queen."

My gut told me something was very wrong. "We're going to the hospital," I said. I handed Andrew to *The Prince* and quickly put on some clothes. Minutes later, *The Prince* was in a panic as well. "He's dying!" he said. **I didn't have the luxury of breaking down.** I needed to get my baby to the hospital, quickly.

As *The Prince* drove, I held Andrew to my chest to feel his heartbeat. He remained limp. Sometimes he stirred. At the hospital, I rushed Andrew into the ER.

A nurse placed him on a gurney and strapped him to a machine to check his vitals. Immediately, he stopped breathing. Doctors worked on him, but no one would tell me what was wrong. I watched in horror as all those doctors surrounded my previously healthy son. He seemed too small to endure so much.

How had this happened? Just yesterday he was active and full of life and now he was barely alive. On my watch, I watched the seconds tick by while Andrew lay there without breathing. The doctors revived him, but then his heart began to beat too quickly. They then worked to slow his heart rate. Instead, it stopped again. If he made it, he might suffer irreversible brain damage.

My bright, energetic, curious boy could end up in a vegetative state, or with impaired mental or physical functioning. The doctors looked at me. I needed to decide how long they should keep working to keep Andrew alive.

I looked at *The Prince*. "What should we do?" He shook his head. "You decide."

I felt completely alone and angry at his not taking any responsibility for the decision, especially considering he was a medical doctor. The doctors continued to work on Andrew. Although he was on oxygen, it took a while, before his heart began to beat again.

At least a dozen medical professionals were in the room, rushing around, punching buttons on machines, and sticking needles into my baby. I heard uncertainty in their voices. They didn't know what was wrong with him, and so they didn't know how to save him. They worked frantically, but his heart was still racing. Every time they got him stabilized, his heart rate went back up. No one could figure out why.

Andrew stopped breathing several times. He was technically dead more than once. They repeatedly revived him. Each time his heart would race up to 250+ beats per minute, then it would stop beating. During this chaos, the toxicology report came back. Andrew had a near lethal dose of amitriptyline, known as Elavil in his bloodstream.

When we'd first brought him in, they'd asked if he'd ingested something that might cause heart failure, or maybe an allergic reaction. I thought back over the past twenty-four hours. He hadn't eaten anything unusual.

Carolyn arrived at the hospital. I asked her if she had given Andrew anything. "Baby aspirin, for his teething. Something I often do before bedtime," she replied. I turned back to the doctor, "Could that be it?" He shook his head, "It must be something else."

I thought of the many people in and out of the house. Did someone give him something? I couldn't imagine it. It made no sense. The toxicology report said that Andrew had been given a near lethal dose of amitriptyline.

"What is that?" I asked. "An antidepressant, commonly prescribed for depression in middle-aged adults," the doctor said. "Where would Andrew get such a thing?" I asked.

"One child I know ingested half the amount …. and that child didn't survive," the doctor said. He saw the shock on my face. "The only hope," he added, "is to filter the poison from his body."

"Poison?" I was shocked.

The doctors pumped Andrew's tiny body full of charcoal. His body distended and convulsed in spasms. The charcoal settled into his fatty tissues, to pull the poison from his vital organs. One doctor said, "It's like filling his surrounding organs with charcoal cement." It was terrifying to watch my baby suffer so profoundly. After watching him suffer for four hours, I said in distress, "Remove the tubes. I wouldn't do this to an animal. Let me hold him." I couldn't let Andrew die this way, in such agony. I took him and held him to my chest thinking it would be the last time. In my arms, his heartbeat slowed. His cries subsided. Then a doctor said, "He's improving."

The charcoal was working. Andrew's little body was trying to live. He began to breathe on his own. Now my own heart was racing, and I started to think more clearly.

"I don't take this medication. Where would he get such a thing?" I asked the doctor. Even as I said it, I knew. Carolyn hadn't given Andrew aspirin, she had given him Elavil.

I couldn't prove the Elavil belonged to Carolyn. She accused Michelle of giving it to Andrew, even though teenagers did not use that drug.

The Child Advocacy team at the hospital concluded that Carolyn was to blame. She was the only one with access during the time the drug was administered, and the only person who fit the profile of someone who would take Elavil. This was no accident. Andrew didn't have the fine motor skills to grasp a pill and bring it to his mouth. In trying to keep Andrew quiet that night, she had almost killed him.

Andrew wasn't the same after we brought him home. He wasn't lively or curious, and he had stopped crawling. The doctors didn't know what to expect. "His brain was deprived of oxygen. He might be severely delayed, or he might fully recover. He might have delayed motor skills, difficulty crawling, an inability to grasp objects, problems with concentration, and mental and intellectual delays."

I knew what that felt like. I would do everything I could to help Andrew grow up healthy and strong. As soon as he was discharged from the hospital, I took him to an educational therapist twice a week, to help him reach the ordinary milestones of childhood.

His brain was still young and malleable. I wouldn't leave his future to chance. I took to heart the positive prediction of his doctors, "that he might recover", and rejected their negative ones. I hired tutors and special education teachers immediately. I enrolled him in preschool as soon as possible. I wanted to give him every opportunity for a bright future, and did not want Carolyn's actions to deprive him of that.

I fired Carolyn and began an investigation. I dug into her life. Why hadn't the system weeded her out? Why had she been highly recommended?

I went to her apartment, and confronted her. I called the nanny agency. I had *The Prince* call her doctor to find out if Carolyn had a prescription for Elavil. All I could think was if she did this to my child, she could do it to someone else's child.

The law WAS NOT on my side. I tried to subpoena her medical records, but medical privacy was sacrosanct back then.

I discovered that the agency had sent me a fraud. Carolyn was not who she claimed to be. She had not graduated from Tuskegee College. Her social security number was fake. Most alarming of all, she'd had an infant herself who had died of unknown causes, and her husband had also died under suspicious circumstances.

The law and the agency had failed me and Andrew. They had not conducted a background check. They had never even checked her references. The more I dug, the more I uncovered. Carolyn had been in and out of psychiatric care her entire adult life. She had been diagnosed with chronic depression (which was why she was on Elavil). How had she become a nanny? How had she made it through the system?

I could not let this go. I called the Child Advocacy investigators and the police. Carolyn needed to be held responsible for the harm she'd done. I pushed for criminal charges against her. I was ignored by law enforcement. Without an eyewitness, I couldn't prove she had deliberately harmed my child.

Denver Post article about Carolyn, 1991

I didn't give up. I sued the agency. They settled out of court. I could have kept fighting, but it wouldn't have made any difference. This woman had nearly killed my child but "the burden of proof" was on me. The law and the licensing organizations didn't seem to care about protecting vulnerable children. They had no time to even try and improve this flawed system, but I did.

There were no standards for screening childcare professionals at the time. It was more difficult to become a beautician, real estate agent, or a beekeeper than a nanny or daycare worker. I met other women whose children had also been abused or even killed by their childcare providers.

These women and I were advocates for change. My son, Andrew was poisoned by his nanny, Judith Englehart's young daughter had been molested at a licensed daycare facility, Debra's eleven-month-old son had died after head injuries at a daycare, and Norma McKinnon's daughter was shaken so hard that she suffered severe brain damage and partial blindness. This once perfectly healthy nine-month-old would be a vegetable for the rest of her life. These mothers and myself had entrusted our children to people who were supposed to be trained to provide childcare in a safe environment. Instead, many of these people were never qualified.

There were no federal standards, and state regulations varied widely.

Police could trace a stolen car across state lines, but not stop a person convicted of child abuse in one state from setting up a daycare in another.

There were regulations for cleaning washcloths at a daycare, but no requirements for background checks. There were numerous laws about animal abuse, but almost none for the abuse of children in daycare or by nannies. It was outrageous.

Law enforcement, the judicial system, and the psychiatric community often blamed the mothers instead of these abusers: for not staying home; for turning our children's care over to someone else; and for stepping outside the accepted roles of wife and mother.

I had learned, often a woman has no other choice. She needs to work, to earn the income, as well as to feel valued outside the home. She shouldn't be punished. **And the children shouldn't be abused, for any reason.**

**In 1988, Public Awareness About Abuse in Child Care (PAACC) was formed to change the system and educate the public.** It was formed by three women: Norma McKinnon, Judith Englehart and myself—it was a nonprofit that had a clear mission: to protect children.

We lobbied state and federal lawmakers for consistent, tough minimum regulations for daycare facilities and in home childcare providers. We worked to raise awareness about the prevalence of child abuse at the hands of said providers. We served as a support group for mothers whose children had been harmed while in daycare or by a nanny.

Within the first year, we worked with the Colorado State Board of Social Services to enact regulations that would require any adult with access to children in a childcare setting to undergo a background and fingerprinting check through the Colorado Bureau of Investigation (CBI), and to register with a central registry. We pushed for increased licensing specialists within the state and for granting social services the power to levy fines on childcare providers found to be in violation of these rules.

Social service agencies were on board. Now we needed the force of the law behind us. We visited the offices of every state representative and senator in Colorado. One lawmaker said, "What do you expect, a perfect system?" And many stated that women belonged at home.... problem solved. **It was disheartening how easily women were dismissed.** Another representative, Betty Neale (D), sponsored a bill to turn the fingerprinting and background check requirements into state law. Unfortunately, Rep. John Webber (R) filibustered the bill and it never came to a vote. The people working against us were childcare providers and nanny agencies, because they did not want to pay a fee for a background check or a license.

We wanted the help of the media, but the editor of the Rocky Mountain

News said, "Go home and take care of your children. If you'd been doing that all along, none of this would have happened." We heard this a lot, especially from men.

I fortunately decided to stop at the desk of a female reporter, Verna Jones. She listened and was sympathetic. "I have three kids myself, but I'm not sure there's anything I can do."

"Where are they right now?" I asked.

"In daycare," she responded automatically. Then her eyes opened with

PLUS: FASHION/BARING IT ALL - Page 14 | DAVID MCQUAY/GAY FRIENDS - Page 2

# CONTEMPORARY

## WHO'S WATCHING OUR CHILDREN?

Denice Reich's crusade to make day care safe

THE SUNDAY DENVER POST                                    APRIL 30, 1989

Denver Post feature, 1989

the realization of what that might mean.

"You have to do something to help," I said. "Your children's lives are literally at stake."

I showed her my research and the statistics: story after story of children being abused, molested, disabled, permanently injured, and even killed by childcare providers.

She wrote an in depth front page feature titled, "Who Is Caring for the Children in Colorado?" Her story was on the front page of The Wall Street Journal and was picked up by other national publications.

We were on the map. PAACC was a small organization. We were only three women working the phones.

Then I got a call from a reporter at The Wall Street Journal. "I just read that you're going to be on Oprah tomorrow."

"What?" I said. I decided to go home early the next day to watch the Oprah Winfrey show to see what they were talking about".

A group of women from California, whose children also had been harmed by childcare providers, part of an organization, Parents Against Child Abuse (PACA) were on. To my shock, one of the mothers was actually wearing the same dress I had on that day. Her child had been also given Elavil by a nanny, but she had died – the child's name was Ashley Sneed. When Oprah asked one of the mothers, Sherri Robertson, who had a child that had been shaken at daycare, what was the name of their group, and when did they start, she stated it was PACA (Parents Against Child Abuse), and the start date was the exact date we had started our organization in Colorado. I was in disbelief. When she interviewed the last mother, whose child had been molested in daycare, I picked up the phone, and asked the operator how to get in touch with the Oprah Winfrey show. Eventually, I was connected by the producers of the show to Sherri Robertson. We bonded over our similar experiences.

The result: we joined forces. Suddenly, we were all on 48 Hours, Donahue, Joan Rivers, and Larry King Live.

Bernie Goldberg, from 48 hours actually personally visited the families from Colorado that had been affected by this crisis, and gave an in-depth report.

His report helped to expose the childcare crisis. I learned that child abusers count on the silence of their victims. **Very young children unable to articulate what has happened to them, and even older children can easily be coerced into silence.** For that reason, child abusers would accept childcare work, and were accepted for jobs, regardless of their history. Everywhere I turned, the system was designed and resistant to furthering the protection of children.

We wouldn't be silenced. We printed flyers and placed advertisements about the dangers of shaking a baby. We raised awareness about the lack of oversight in childcare facilities. I demanded a grand jury investigation, with the help of Ginger Law and Dianne Balkin. I remain deeply grateful for their tireless commitment. Steve Siegel with the District Attorney's office encouraged me to keep fighting, saying to me, "If it's meant to be, it's up to me."

The law had an immediate impact. In the first months, ninety-six of the registered childcare providers were discovered to have criminal records, including arrests for driving under the influence, sexual assault, and murder. Still to this day, every year the testing by the Colorado Bureau of Investigation reveals 90-100 felons per 1,000 tested.

We were making a difference, but it wasn't enough. Abuse in childcare settings was a nationwide problem. We needed federal oversight and regulation. I testified at a Senate hearing in Washington, D.C., and was asked by one senator, "Why did you let someone else care for your child?" **that was the mentality at the time.**

For four years, I didn't sleep more than a few hours a night. I woke up every day with determination, and went to sleep with nagging questions, **"How could a system be so lacking in common sense and so inept?" These were not objects we were fighting for, we were fighting to protect the future.** Nothing was more important to me than fighting the system that had almost killed my baby.

If I had been fighting alone, I may have given up. But together with these women who had suffered a similar fate or worse, we were strong.

The longer we talked about what had happened to us, the more other mothers would come forward and join the cause. As women, we had been taught to be quiet and ladylike. We were not supposed to speak up or out. We ignored the negativity. We were fighting for all the children.

We had two choices when our children were abused or killed by the people we had hired to care for them: We could be victims, or we could be warriors. We went to war against the institutions and the people who sought to protect the the childcare system.

We had no idea how difficult it would be to get a bill passed to protect children.We didn't have the resources to hire a professional lobbyist (at the time the minimum retainer to hire a lobbyist was $14,000), so we decided to be our own lobbyist, and try and bring the filibustered bill back to the House floor.

We started at the top, because we felt we did not have the time to delay such an important issue at stake. We pushed our way into Rep. Tillie Bishop's (R) office, who was well known for his compassion. It was difficult to explain the issue broadly, so Judith Englehart told him the story of her daughter, and how she had been sexually molested at a licensed daycare (still operating today). He was moved to tears by her story, and ended up cosponsoring the bill with Rep. Neal. With bipartisan support, the bill became law.

We didn't win every battle, and there are still problems in the system, but we did make a difference. We raised awareness of an issue that hadn't been widely discussed before. We insisted that the media and the lawmakers stop blaming mothers for working. We raised our voices. We demanded to be taken seriously on the issue of childcare safety.

People also started educating themselves about the dangers of shaking a baby, and the resulting Shaken Baby Syndrome. I even paid for an ad to show what happens to a baby's brain if they are shaken – the same end result as throwing an egg off the roof of a two-story building. If life had taught me anything, it was that nothing will happen unless I make it happen.

**When the world puts a roadblock in your path, this I know to be true:**
*Don't lie down.*
*Don't give up.*
*Don't turn around.*
*Find a way to go over, around, or through every obstacle.*

Accepting the Unacceptable

# 7

# After Failure Comes the Next Solution

Family Court and the Reality of Loss

After two decades, I came to the realization that no matter how hard I tried to please *The Prince*, he would always have affairs, and be a sadistic adversary. I knew he was obsessed with the power of intimidation. To survive in the marriage, I used my humor. The children and I had insulated the whole attic of our house, and it was not a great idea. I should have just called someone who specialized in "blowing in" insulation instead of the children and I attempting such an itchy project. After that fiasco, I put a bucket of the itchy insulation in the laundry room, and did a load of *the Prince's* underwear. After the laundry was clean, I turned the underwear inside out and rubbed it in the crotch area. Every time I watched him itch, I would laugh inside. **He never said anything to me, because he assumed he was itching from the affair he was having. He never realized you can't ride two horses with one ass, and pretend nothing has changed.**

He used a hair growth product daily since he was going bald. I replaced the liquid hair growth product, with a hair removal product, which he diligently massaged into his scalp. I would watch him wondering why it wasn't working.

Obviously this did not make up for his years of abuse, but it was a small victory against an abuser, and that made me smile.

He was always worried about maintaining the status quo, and would only buy expensive items (even when we had no money for them). He was embarrassed by my estate and garage sale shopping.

I had a friend who owned the Keystone Pawn Shop. They had an Omega watch in, and I knew *the Prince* wanted one. I could never had afforded it new, and was excited to purchase this one for his birthday. Unfortunately, I did not realize it was engraved – the engraving read, "Willie West, King Soopers." It was still a very nice Omega watch, but he never wore it, and was very angry I had purchased a "used" item for him. I should have known, because previously I had picked up some Brooks Brothers suits from an estate sale (his size, the brand of suit he preferred, and in perfect condition), and he refused to wear them. I realized that the only possible next step was to stop my own behavior of trying to please him.

**I no longer tried or expressed my emotions around him, I just stayed silent and made him invisible.** I was done with his needless spending, violence, confusing lies, terrifying rants, and many affairs.

I filed for divorce. Andrew was four, Kay twelve, Michelle eighteen and a senior in high school. Maura was twenty-two and had reconnected with her birth mother and moved to California. It was painful for me to be so discounted since her birth mother had abandoned her years before, and I had raised her.

Before moving out, *the Prince* exerted his control one last time. He made sure my driver's license was revoked due to my previous head injury (from 32 years ago). Although he never thought this was an issue in the almost twenty years of our marriage when I was responsible for driving the children to 3 different schools (one was an 88 mile round-trip), driving them to all of their extracurricular activities, driving to work every day to support our family, and driving for all the household and shopping concerns. I had an impeccable driving record, this made no sense, but he was successful in having my license revoked. He did this hoping I would lose my job without a car. *The Prince* was so angry with me for finally asking for the divorce to reclaim my independence, that he would do anything to break me. He thought this would ruin my career.

Once again, he underestimated me. He no longer had the ability to manipulate me, because I was now thinking for myself.

Until I was able to reinstate my license, I started riding an old bicycle to my listings since I was unable to drive. Wearing my best suit and heels, I pedaled up and down a major city thoroughfare, through rain, snow, and heat. My work was the key to my independence, and I was determined to succeed. One day when it was heavily sleeting and very cold, I decided enough was enough and just started driving my car again. Towards the end of the first week, I was late for a closing and didn't realize I had been speeding. A young police officer in Glendale pulled me over. I was panicked. I had no driver's license or insurance. I was desperate because he asked to see those documents, and I would lose everything if I let him know that I didn't have them. Thinking fast, I said I was having a miscarriage, and I didn't want to embarrass him or myself by getting my purse out of the back of the car. I then told him I needed to get to the hospital, because the blood clots were coming out like,"meat liver". His face turned beet red, and he asked if I would like an escort to the hospital. I said, "No, I am just going to Rose Medical Center, and I know where it is." I then asked if it was ok to leave, and he said yes. **Sometimes you just have to create your own miracle.** I knew was lucky, and that young policeman had no idea the impact he made in my life."

I was naïve thinking we would not separate completely. I thought we would occasionally get together as a family. I thought we would both be happier. I was wrong. His anger at the divorce consumed him. I never imagined that I would be entering the most difficult decade of my life. After I filed, *The Prince* told me he would "ruin me." He would also go for sole custody, and I would lose everything. "I will make it so tough for you that either you will kill yourself or you'll be ready for a mental hospital."

Unfortunately, I believed in the justice system to be fair. I hired "the best divorce attorney", who told me *The Prince's* attorney had no experience as a divorce attorney, that he was only a criminal attorney. During the process, I discovered that my attorney had not been filing papers at all. Because of this, I received several contempt of court charges. Concerned, I would call about these, and he always arrogantly replied, "he knew what he was doing." He was not engaged in my case at all, and I did not understand why. He was also losing his hair at an alarming rate. When I questioned him about it, he replied, "It was nothing." Turns out he had terminal brain cancer and died a week before my trial.

I needed to scramble to hire another attorney. The next attorney I hired was equally dismissive of me. I rationalized that was how attorneys conducted themselves. I later realized they are often there just to sell their hours, while functioning under the myth of protecting you. Another layer that made it so difficult was the *Prince* hiring a criminal attorney for a family court proceeding. It did not have the atmosphere of family court, but an actual criminal trial, and I was the defendent. The whole process is overwhelming, and difficult to navigate.

*The Prince's* attorney picked the judge (who was retired) to preside over the case. He had been friends and colleagues with this judge earlier in their careers, when both were Assistant District Attorneys. My second attorney seemed unable to keep pace with *The Prince's* criminal attorney and hand-picked judge. When I questioned him about this, he replied, "He was not going to be my attorney for much longer since he was sick." Turns out he also had cancer, and before he even presented my case in court, my second attorney had died.

I began to feel defeated, and exhausted. It felt like I was being punished for my past medical history, as well as for being the primary breadwinner. The bills were unrelenting, and the judge often fell asleep while my attorney was speaking. I realized that my anger, exhaustion, and humor would have no place in this courtroom. A woman was expected to be docile, not showing any emotions, even though her entire life and that of her children were at stake. It is a frightening experience knowing you have done nothing wrong, yet you could lose everything. Family court can be obscenely unfair if one party is out to just punish the other.

Having to hire another attorney was overwhelming. This attorney was kind and accessible. She did her best to represent me. Even with her sincere desire to level the playing field, I was still held in contempt when I was five hours late bringing Andrew to *The Prince's* home because we were stuck behind a fatal accident on "Dead Man's Curve" (before cell phones, so I could not call). She tried her best to show that it was unavoidable, even presenting a newspaper article on the accident, but I was still held in contempt by the magistrate and could either pay a $3,000 fine or go to jail. It was Mother's Day weekend, so I had to stay 3 days. I didn't have the money, so I said to my attorney, "What more can they do to me?" I accepted it, tried to learn from the experience, and went to jail. **I understood why recidivism was so high after my stay – there were no educational materials there to support women to get out of their pattern of defeat.**

My attorney was so distressed by the justice system after I was held in contempt, she stated, "I can't believe this. It is all so wrong." I let her know that I had come to accept the lack of justice in the system.

Two weeks later, my third attorney was dead. She committed suicide. *The Prince's* attorney actually said, "I was so damaged that I couldn't even keep an attorney" – somehow implying that I was to blame for my attorney's deaths. A few weeks after I was released from county jail on the contempt charge, and my attorney had died, I was called to jury duty. I had to take Andrew with me. Before we went into the courthouse, I told him it was the only place he was ever allowed to lie - because you were punished by the justice system for telling the truth. In my experience, the liars were the ones rewarded in court. Andrew sat on a bench outside the courtroom, and waited for me. The judge walked in, and twirled in a circle, robes and all as a greeting for the potential jurists. It was a very inappropriate display of his self-perceived importance. I just kept reading the newspaper after his entrance, because I was so disgusted with the whole system. He interrupted my reading to say, "Denice Reich is that you?" because we had known each other for years. I was well aware of his bad reputation in his private life. He then asked me (as an example to the other potential jurists) if I would be prejudiced if chosen to serve on the jury. I told him, "I believe so, because I can not tell which attorney lies better than the other." He then told the other potential jurists that my answer was because of my son being poisoned, and the difficulty to receive justice in the case, and that they should disregard my answer. I replied, "It has nothing to do with that. In fact, my son is sitting on a bench outside this room, and I told him when we were entering the courthouse that this was the only place it was acceptable to lie." The judge turned red, and ordered me out of his courtroom. I was happy to make my point, and also to not serve this broken system.

My family court trial was endless. There were a siege of forensic accountants who were keeping tabs on any business I conducted during the trial. I had to copy every file from when I first received my real estate license, until present day. The bills from the attorneys were also overwhelming. They made no sense, but needed to be paid immediately. If you questioned or argued the charges, you were threatened. Here is a humorous example of what the charges were like:

Attorney fee joke

Retainer Fee: $5,000 - Consultant Fee: $3,000 - Negotiation Fee: $3,500 - Processing Fee: $2,000 - Access Fee: $600 - Phone Call Fee: $1,000 - Computer Fee: $1,500 - Fee Fee: $200 - Fee Fi Fo Fum Fee: $150 - Might as Well Fee: $200 - Because we can Fee: $500 - What are you gonna do Fee: $375, and Another Dollar won't hurt Fee: $1. It is cathartic to make fun of it now, but it was no laughing matter at the time.

They went after my home, and everything I inherited from my family in Aspen. This wore me down. The endless meetings with the custody evaluator, accountants, and psychiatrist were overwhelming. Of course I was psychologically depressed by how easily he was able to use the law against me, and how hard it was for me to use the law to protect myself. The judge ignored that I was working full-time while *the Prince* rarely worked, and was usually playing golf. I kept expecting the judge to say, "Enough is enough – you've gone too far - don't expect your soon to be ex-wife to pay for everything, and be the only one held accountable for anything, while you rarely work as a surgeon, and are usually playing golf," but he never did. At the time, I was running a national organization childcare safety, a successful real estate business, and was the only person taking care of the two children still at home. The stress and financial burdens were immense.

I was unable to overcome his façade of being "Father of the Year." Expert witnesses were testifying against me, without ever meeting me. The court never acknowledged that I was the primary breadwinner, primary care-giver of the children, and primary person who ran the household. All of these accomplishments were "invisible" to the process. **This was expected of a woman, and no credit was afforded to me.**

The fact that I was the primary breadwinner was also not a credit to me, but a bonus for *The Prince*, as the forensic accountants made sure to document everything, so *the Prince* would get a larger payout from me, if the case went his way. The court case was so one-sided, that even when *The Prince* admitted to hitting me and hitting the nanny (an incident he was charged with by the police, summoned to court, but after 13 continua-tions, dismissed somehow), he still came out on top. He told the court that although he had hit the nanny and battered me, he was taking an anger management class, and working on getting his temper under control.

He received accolades from the court, for his actions in taking this class, yet no censure for the abuse. His crimes against me and the nanny were trivialized. If it wasn't so unfair, it would be laughable. One time he even called my office and told the receptionist, "Let everyone know that Denice Reich is being nominated for Woman of the Year by the Epilepsy Foundation." He was disclosing my personal medical history to my work, trying to shame me, and perhaps have me fired. This helped me see who I was really dealing with. The court did not care. All of my actions for the good of the marriage, children, and family were minimized. **I began to realize that women had no ability to to be heard if a man wanted to deny them custody.** After the death of my third attorney, I hired a fourth attorney. He joked, " I hope I live through to the conclusion."

All my years of stability were overshadowed by *the court considering the status of a doctor above reproach.*

I did not respond well to the lies and accusations leveled against me, instead expressing outrage and displaying humor at the situation. That did not bode well for my case as anger and humor are not perceived as appropriate in a courtroom, but lies are.

I thought it would never end.

It seemed to me this was about which attorney presented their case better, and who the judge liked more. I was shocked that easily disproved lies were being accepted as truths in a courtroom. My attorney often looked defeated, and did not protect me.

*The Prince* fought me at every turn. We were in court for years. The delaying and forensic accounting was so laughable, that when *The Prince* requested I pay him for the cemetery plots, that I had purchased for my parents, I finally sent him a "gift certificate" from Dr. Kevorkian (a well-known advocate for assisted suicide), and included an expiration date of just a few days after I sent it.

In the middle of these proceedings, there were a few other moments of laughter. Once, *The Prince's* lawyer asked me to state my real name and I responded, "Cunt Reich," because I knew that's what *The Prince* often called me. Another time *the Prince's* lawyer kept aggressively pointing his finger in my face. I asked him to stop, and he would not. I finally said to him, "It is really disturbing, because your fly is undone." It wasn't, but he moved his finger away from my face, and to his crotch. No one laughed, they just said I did not get the "seriousness" of the courtroom.

The court required me (but not *the Prince*) to see a psychiatrist, and because I would do anything to keep Andrew and Kay, I made an appointment, believing the sessions were confidential. They were not. Later I discovered that I was not legally bound to go to a custody evaluator since I was the one who always took care of the children, and they had not been abused in any way. No one told me this, they just railroaded me into a situation where there was a predetermined outcome.

The psychiatrist referred to me to was affiliated with the University of Colorado Medical School, and often testified as an "expert witness" for the court system, earning $1,800/day.

**I thought she was required to maintain my privacy,** so when she asked me, "What was the happiest moment in your marriage?" I again used my humor, and told her about the only time I had fought back in my marriage by grabbing *The Prince* by the privates. When she asked me if I regretted grabbing him, I quickly said, "Yes. I regret that I didn't grab him with my right hand, because then I could have done some real damage." I was laughing while telling this story, clearly joking, but she just continued taking notes.

Later, at the court hearing for custody, she testified against me, using this story. I had expectations of privacy and confidentiality that is inferred when seeing a medical professional. I never would have met with her if I knew these sessions were not private. I definitely wouldn't have shared my humor, my anger, depression, vulnerabilities, and fears.

All of it was laid out as "evidence" against me. I assumed the psychiatrist was there in a professional capacity, to help me navigate the proceedings,

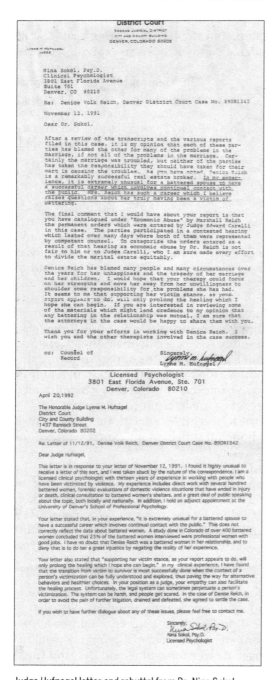

Judge Hufnagel letter and rebuttal from Dr. Nina Sokel

and help facilitate a smooth divorce/custody agreement.

**Anything you say in a custody evaluation can be used against you.** No one informed me this was the case – not the psychiatrist, judge, or even my own lawyer. Obviously, I became very distrustful of the entire process.

Everything *the Prince* said was treated as truth even though he lied like he was breathing oxygen. Nothing I said was taken seriously. *The Prince's* attorney solicited an opinion from Judge Hufnagel, a judge who was not involved in my case. She dismissed my proof of abuse, stating, "You don't fit the profile of a battered wife. You are too successful." In her opinion, Judge Hufnagel wrote, "Denice Reich is a remarkably successful real estate broker. In my experience, it is extremely unusual for a battered spouse to have a successful career that involves continual contact with the public. Mrs. Reich has such a career which, I believe, raises questions about her truly having been a victim of battering."

This judge, with no ties to the proceedings, had based her opinion on nothing more than her personal belief that "successful" women are never victims of battering, in contradiction to evidence provided to the court, and *the Prince's* own admission of battery. At the time, I joined a battered women's group with a gynecologist, a former city councilwoman, an attorney, and an appraiser – all successful, all working with the public, and all battered.

I decided to seek another legal opinion for the court. Dr. Nina Sokel, a psychologist who specialized in treating battered women, recognized my situation for what it was and wrote to Judge Hufnagel, explaining that battered women certainly can be successful businesswomen. Ultimately, the judge retained her opinion as fact and disregarded Dr. Sokel's years of experience with battered women, and differing conclusion. Years later I found the courage to have some of the "medical/custody" experts censured for their behavior. These letters are on the pages at the conclusion of this chapter. This was my only option in bringing a measure of sanity to what had taken place.

For me it was a time of incredible stress. I was multi-tasking a successful real estate business, advocating locally and nationally for childcare system overhaul (even appearing on Larry King, Oprah Winfrey, and other nationally syndicated shows), I was the only parent responsible for running the household and the only parent responsible for all childcare issues for our two children, who were still at home, all while trying to navigate a frightening court system. All of this was dismissed, and the only emphasis was on my medical issues that occurred 32 years prior to the proceedings.

The "expert witness", Dr. K, that I had hired through the recommendation of the court, chose to ignore that I had been given 800mg of Thorazine (twice the threshold dose), which lowered the seizure threshold in my youth. Instead of this, she just emphasized this 30+ year old information of seizures, not the side effects of this overmedicating, and not acknowledging my impeccable, successful, stable life after that time, both as a parent and in the workforce. I held the same job, at the same company, and, in fact, still work for them 30 years later.

I had to reschedule one of our appointments because I was appearing on Larry King, representing PAACC, and in the next session Dr. K commented to me that she had written, "numerous scientific papers, and never been asked to speak on a nationally syndicated show." The papers were not on the childcare issues, so I was not sure why she stated this. I explained to her that it was not some "romantic" thing, but something I was doing to try and protect children. I always felt she harbored jealousy after this and became even more critical of me.

She further prescribed Prozac during this time, stating I was "depressed." Obviously I was depressed, I was being attacked economically, and being threatened with the loss of my children. **The most**

**dangerous person you can see might be a psychiatrist.** Often you will be prescribed damaging drugs, or they will have the power to "lock you up" without a jury. Dr. Wilets, (the second custody evaluator, who was a medical doctor – the first evaluator was not), also stated that the fact I had been depressed was normal in such an abnormal situation. "Of course anyone would be depressed in these circumstances." He felt Prozac never should have been prescribed.

Even though Dr. Wilets (that the court allowed me to hire because of bias from the first) stated I was a "high functioning woman, who had an incredible internal drive to go forward,….that I was aware of my strengths and weaknesses…….and that I was a woman of substantial success and achievements", and that he was, "Struck by the emphasis that Jean Lacrosse put on the negative features pointed out in the report about Denice.", his opinions were discarded in favor of the first evaluator's biased opinions.

This first evaluator (JL) had an agenda and a long history of being a "hired gun" for attorney's with male clients seeking custody. All of her predictions about myself suddenly becoming unsuccessful (after years of success), or becoming incapacitated (based on overmedication from 30 + years ago), or that I could not "adjust" to my new circumstances, or that I was not "good enough" never happened. In fact, it just motivated me to continue on the same path of success in my personal and professional life that I had already been following for decades. **I can not emphasize enough how dangerous these so-called professionals can be when they use their power to forward their own personal agenda.**

One of my major regrets is after successfully getting the other psychiatrist/psychologist censured, I did not have the stomach for another fight. I was just so defeated by the process after my incredible loss.

These people are dangerous. They have the ability to label a person after seeing them for less than a few "sessions." Understand this - twenty years of good parenting, and financial success……less than a few hours for a conclusion that you are an unfit parent that the court takes as "truth." They also make unsubstantiated "predictions" of a person's future actions. These are also taken as evidence by the court. When the future proves them wrong, the victim does not get any relief or apology. **Criminals are treated better in our court system.**

Throughout these proceedings, *The Prince's* performance was worthy of Hollywood. He insisted he'd never been anything but a perfect and loving husband, and he denied continued abuse. Finally, he'd found a venue where his lies served him well. His position as a doctor commanded respect in the courtroom. He painted an alternate narrative that the court took as evidence.

After all of this I shut down, I stopped expressing my opinions.

I stopped talking about my feelings, I trusted no one. **Betrayals**

**silenced me into a calm acceptance of the unacceptable.** There is immense loneliness when you become silent. Silence was my loudest cry that no one would hear, and I remained speechless.

Finally a judge, Stephen Phillips stepped in and ended the nightmare. He started a pilot program so future divorce cases would not be allowed to drag on for years. I am still grateful to him.

My experience with the family court system was far from just. It is a place where families are destroyed. Evidence is manufactured, and truths are often ignored. It is about credentialed "experts" from opposite sides, against each other, with all of them swearing, under oath, their anti-theoretical positions, based on the same set of facts. It is about their personal agendas and opinions, and their own beliefs, that what they say should be taken as the "truth." Because psychiatrists have "diagnosed" you, does not make it the truth. It is often just an opinion from a theory they were taught in school, or because they are just people who make mistakes.

These differing conclusions, based on the same facts, are amplified, and often validated throughout the trial.

The extortion of money, and the party with the most confident and experienced attorney who is the most adept at creating a smoke screen to confuse, mislead or obscure the truth to the court usually winning, is unjust. I can only equate the family court divorce/custody system to organized crime – where finances are extorted, and one parent is destroyed in the falsehood of the "best interests of the children." **Never assume justice is on the side of fairness. The use of power is rarely accompanied by the moral choice.**

Avoid this system. It is a sewer. A circus of unending lies designed to break you down. It does not make it right that you are told, "It's better than other countries." This is not "other countries."

This is America, and the court system should reflect that. Remember, just because you are depressed during divorce/custody proceedings, that is normal because you are often surrounded by unfair practices.

The losing party is often shell-shocked at the injustice and loss. I personally know five women, who were amazing mothers who unfairly lost custody, and were so devastated by the injustice, and were so impoverished both financially and emotionally, they were unable to create a new life.

The children of these women also suffered, not having relationships with their mothers. The court never addressed any of these long-lasting repercussions of their unfair decisions. **Psychiatry and weather forecasting are the only professions I can think of where every failure leads to more profit.**

Andrew was almost six, and Kay was fourteen by the time custody was determined. They had never lived without me, yet the judge ignored all the history and facts, and ruled that I was incapable of raising Andrew and Kay, even though I had been the sole caregiver to both their entire lives, because of my previous medical condition. He then ignored my medical history completely when deciding that I was capable of working fulltime in a professional capacity, awarding an extremely large monthly sum to *the Prince* (for child support and alimony – even though he was a surgeon), and making me "buy him out" of all my assets, including my home, and half of the appreciation of my family property in Aspen, as well as the real estate assets I had purchased for the children's future (which he kept for himself, never returning to the children). It made no sense. My family, friends, and colleagues were shocked. I was also in shock, because my belief that a person is treated fairly in court was ruined. It destroyed my trust of the justice system in America.

I was devastated by so much loss. I had to accept the fact that I had lost everything, and my future for many years would be figuring out how to pay the overwhelming financial judgment(s) against me. I had to be creative - paying some of the bills with an insurance payout meant for a new roof, paying some with the sale of a prized doll, paying by holding garage sales, selling my prized antiques to pay the attorneys. I still try to be the best mother I could be on the two weekends a month afforded to me by the court. **It is hard to let go of the memories of a family that once existed because it was a great story at times, one that you never expected to end.** Sometimes you have to move on from a person, if they are meant to still be in your life, they will either catch up or be left behind with their anger.

Once again in my life, it was not about what had happened to me, but how I chose to get up and create a new future. The strongest action I could take after such defeat was to live my life well. **When the wrong people leave your life, the right things start to happen.**

# 8

# Better You Should Cry Now, Then I Should Cry Later

his is my story and experiences of raising four children in a blended family. It is very different than the fiction that was presented to family court by the *Prince*, and his criminal attorney. The key injustice of being a mother (exploited by the family court) is having to "prove" how much you love your own children, and never getting to speak of the pain, difficulty, and hardship involved in that role but also of the love and wonderful memories involved in that role. No one saw what I did for the children, they only saw what I did not do. **It is not easy being a mother, if it was, fathers would do it.**

Although family court never acknowledged my life as a mother, the fact was that I was a mother who was always present in her children's lives, and who always took care of them, and worked hard to help them become responsible adults.

I was a typical mother, working 24/7 – the only shift offered. Mothers are a social experiment proving sleep is not a crucial part of life. I was not a perfect mother, but there were a million reasons I was a good one. I was the glue of the family, holding everything together. I relished the fact that my children were all so different, with completely differing personalities and agendas. They were born in different decades. **I wanted them to feel loved and be empowered to become successful adults.** I did everything I could because I cared so much for them. My experience is that it is better to be a tough parent while children are young and able to learn, then suffer the consequences of being too easy on them and creating silver spoon kids that feel the world revolves around their needs, not society's needs. Children that have no boundaries become adults with unrealistic expectations of how society should cater to their needs. Parents who entitle their children often create disabled adults. Often times, they are unable to handle the reality of the real world, and will abuse drugs, or make other destructive choices. Therefore, the expression, "Better you should cry now then I should cry later" I feel applies to good parenting.

While they were growing up, I would wake them every morning with the Lee Greenwood song, "I'm proud to be an American." Then they would get ready for school, and if I had a new listing, we would leave early, and they would help me put my real estate flyers under the newspapers that everyone would have on their porches. They would also help me reposition my concrete advertising benches to face rush hour traffic – before school and after school.

The schools in our area were substandard at the time. Maura was in the first grade and was not punished for her bad behavior in the public school system. For example, she would throw pencils at the teacher, and disrupt the entire classroom with no consequences. I knew there was something very wrong with this method of teaching. When speaking with the teachers, I was told that she was "borderline retarded (a term that is no longer used)".

I knew Maura was not "boderline retarded". This was the same child who had plucked a valuable piece of art from a pile of junk. I saw her potential, and felt she was the opposite of their "diagnosis". I had her tested at Children's Hospital of Colorado, and although they confirmed she had a learning disability that would make it difficult to learn in the public school system, she was exceptionally intelligent, and her behavior was because of the system she was in. They suggested I enroll her in a new, private school that had recently opened that would afford her the ability to learn with her disability.

The school was Havern, and they stated that they, "Created Bright Futures for Children with Learning Disabilities." The teacher to student ratio was 4:1 or lower, compared to the public school system which was 30:1 or lower ratio at the time. I felt this was a wonderful solution, and even though I had to drive 88 miles/day for her to attend Havern, I was thrilled to be able to give this opportunity to Maura. *The Prince* did not support this decision, so I paid for 100% of the tuition myself. He wanted to put her in a school for "troubled children" instead. I was shocked that a doctor would not be able to understand what Havern could offer his child.

Because of this experience, my next child, Michelle, was immediately put into private school as well. This was a huge financial burden, and I ended up paying for her private schooling as well by myself. *The Prince* refused to pay, since there was a "free" option. Yet I knew I needed to address the children's education in a more proactive way, to give them the greatest chance of a future. When Kay was ready to enter school, there was a great elementary school in the public school system. I wanted her to have the chance to go there, so I purchased a rental home in that neighborhood, so she was able to attend the school. After she finished elementary school because the middle and high school public schools were still poor in Denver, I put her into private school. She did have some learning disabilities as well, and I realized she also needed this.

When Andrew was ready to start school, I knew any public school or mainstream private school would not be a good fit. I enrolled him in the private school that Maura had attended, Havern, from the start because he needed a lot of extra support because of the trauma he suffered as a child from his nanny. In fact, I ended up hiring a private tutor for all four children to help them with their schooling. People who have good neighborhood public schools do not realize just how lucky they are. I did what I was able to do (by paying private tuitions, driving to different schools every day, and hiring tutors) to give them a good education.

I felt my children needed to learn responsibility and have a strong work ethic, which included chores. Each child will probably handle this differently, and part of the job as a supportive parent is understanding this, and making sure to help them improve, if needed. The key to achieving goals in life is to always show up, on time, and with enthusiasm. Maura and Michelle approached responsibility and the completion of their chores as part of life and acted appropriately. Kay would never do any chore. I needed to try and teach her to take responsibility as well. She needed to learn that she was a part of the family, and act accordingly.

One month, it was her chore to empty the trash. She refused to do this. I decided that every time she refused to take the trash out, I would dump it on the floor of her room, until she took responsibility to take the trash out. This went on for 3 weeks. With 3 weeks of trash on her floor, and Kay not relenting at all, I gave her two choices; I would take out the trash for her if she pulled the weeds in the yard, or if she would dig out the dandelions. Until she either took out the trash or did one of the yard chores, she also would not be allowed to watch M.A.S.H. with the rest of the family (our favorite tv show at that time). She ended up digging up the dandelions (not whole heartedly!), and I took out the trash. I wanted to show her, and the rest of my children that they did not get to just not do their chores.

One time Andrew offered to rake the leaves from a big Oak tree of an older neighbor. He gave her a very low estimate. She accepted – he had to return to her home multiple weekends to complete the job, but was never offered more money, and he never asked for it. He knew that his estimate had been too low but completed the project for the estimate he provided. My lessons with him were a success, he was honest, kind, and kept his word. That experience did not dampen his entrepreneurial spirit. One time during the summer in Aspen, I noticed that Andrew seemed to have a lot of money. I became concerned. Where was this money coming from? Mothers do better research than the FBI, so I confronted him, and he led me to the shed, where he had a giant stack of Playboy magazines he had been selling to the other young men. He had found them in a recycling bin and realized he would be able to earn some money reselling them.

Also, from the time Andrew was three until he turned fourteen, he sold the Aspen Times when we were in Aspen for the summers. It was a valuable lesson in sales, that has helped him to this day. The concept of selling the Aspen Times was where the children of Aspen learned free enterprise, and other life lessons. They had to be among the first to pick up the papers to be competitive. The Aspen Times came out some days as early as 3pm, and many times much later, so the children had to wait in line. The papers were hot off the press, and the kids paid 10cents a paper,

Andrew selling the Aspen Times, 1980s

and sold for whatever the market would bear. Every child anxiously awaited their stack of 10-20 papers, so they could sell in their favorite territory. The papers would still be warm when picked up, and his face and hands would be covered in black ink. In the early years, Andrew would sell to the tourists on the mall, because he was so charming and little (dressed as an old 1920s newspaper boy). I sewed him this outfit, and made sure his knickers had big pockets, so he could put the money in them. When the tourists would ask how much a paper cost, he would reach inside the pockets and show them all the money he had. The tourists would count the money and give him the same amount, or more. In later years, he had his territory at City Market, the largest grocery store in town. He was able to purchase a rental property with the money he earned and saved in later years, since I matched his funds.

Anytime a situation with my children arose where they did not want to complete their chores, I would offer alternatives, but would not cave on them doing something. I realized through this process that if you tell a child something hundreds of times or ask a child to do something multiple times and they still do not understand or complete the task, then it is not the child who is the slow learner.

I was learning to be a mom, too. I did not say, "Great job" for a chore, or an ordinary task. They needed to realize that they were just doing what every responsible person was doing. If they ever complained about being "bored", I immediately found them a chore to do. It did not take them long to stop complaining. The same went for boundaries. If they complained or were angry when you set a boundary, it just meant that boundary was necessary.

Children need to develop a tolerance for disappointment, and an ability to solve problems without being paralyzed by the fear of the problem. I did not emphasize grades, but rather the fact that they worked hard at school, using their skills to the highest degree possible. It was a continuation of the book I always read to them growing up, "The Little Engine that Could.", and I would repeat to them, "I think I can, I think I can..." whenever they needed extra encouragement. I let them know, however, that they were responsible for their own choices.

I was determined to guide them to be the best they could be. I wanted them to avoid the "victim" mentality, which was a roadblock to their future. **The world does not reward whining, only accomplishments.** I also taught this through my own life – I knew most problems were solvable, and I showed them how a person could solve problems and multitask while doing so.

I taught them money management as well, so they didn't think they were able to just purchase anything they wanted. I wanted them to understand the value of money.

My lessons and projects were not always successful. One time when they all wanted down comforters, I took them to the thrift store, and we purchased everything we could find that was down filled. We used a vacuum cleaner to get the down feathers out of each item. Our plan was to then empty the full bag of down feathers into a shop vac and use that shop vac to "blow" them into the comforters we were going to make. Before we could do this, the vacuum bag exploded, and there were down feathers everywhere. In our eyes, our noses, our throats. We could hardly see each other. We were sneezing and coughing. We just laughed and laughed, which just made us cough more. It was not a successful project, but everyone did learn.

Aspen for me and the children was always wonderful freedom and adventure. We would float down the salvation ditch in inner tubes, days later we would go to the recycle bin to get magazines and other great reading material. It would be enough for the rest of the summer - we never had to buy any. At night, we would go up to the construction sites on Red Mountain where they were building the new, huge houses. We would use the worker's sawhorses, and put a dining room table together - then we would eat, taking in the extraordinary views. We would laugh and giggle that we had dinner at every McMansion built during our summers in Aspen.

We would hike to the grottos to look at the naked free spirited people on the rocks, sunbathing. We would then arrive in our neighborhood, where Katherine, a potter, also lived. She would make vases also while naked. She was an attraction, and all of our joking aside, her pieces were extraordinary. We also used to go to garage sales, where we would find treasures, and consignment shops, where we would purchase things like front doors at great prices.

As Aspen became more wealthy, unfortunately, the recycle bins no longer exist, the construction sites are all closed, children no longer sell the Aspen Times, and garage sales and consignment shops are few. The restaurants have been replaced with places that are so expensive, that a regular person is not able to go. Also, all the fun and quirkiness of Aspen in their buildings and lawns has also disappeared thanks to the City of Aspen's government regulating everything to their taste - and allowing people who purchased historically protected, original Victorian dwellings to build large "ship-like" buildings with tons of square footage.

One of the lessons was that happiness and joy are also part of childhood. If you are able, help your children embrace this. The child who embraced this the most in our house was Michelle. She was like a ray of sunshine, always cheerful. Her laughter filled our days and brought joy to everyone. I avoided letting them watch violent movies or play violent video games. I feel this is a huge problem in our society, and teaches children to become unaffected by violence, and not understand the true consequences of it.

I took them to a furniture store to show them the difference between saving up money to buy a couch, versus the instant gratification of buying it immediately on credit – and how much more that would end up making the couch cost. I also tried to impart to them that "labels" on clothing really meant nothing, and they were not worth the price.

I wanted them to realize that they were responsible for their actions and choices – not just with money management, but with all life's decisions. They did not fare well by blaming others and needed to take personal responsibility.

At birthday parties, I saw extravagant gifts being given. Often the receivers of these gifts became overwhelmed and overstimulated. One time I gave a watch to a neighborhood boy at his Bar Mitzvah. It seemed extravagant to me at the time. He took one look at it, threw it on the floor and said, "I already have this." I could not believe the rudeness. I picked it up off the floor and returned it. I decided I would use the money I had spent on that gift on someone who would appreciate it.

After a birthday party, Michelle came home crying – holding the gift in her hand that she had picked out to give the birthday child. When I asked her why she still had the gift, and why she had not given it to the child, she said, "The mother of the birthday child gave the same gift as a party favor to all the children." That same mother latched onto Michelle as her child's best friend and took her skiing. Michelle came home with very expensive skis and ski clothing that was purchased for her by the mother of the child. I made Michelle immediately return these items. Just because the other mother had no idea of the value of teaching her children money management and integrity, did not mean I would "toe her line" and do the same. These children had been taught they were the center of the universe, and expected everything for nothing, and felt they could do no wrong. They would brag about "my wealth" (just their parent's wealth) as if they had earned it themselves. **I did not want my children's future to be destroyed by a sense of entitlement.**

I did not give their children everything they wanted. I knew it made them demanding, and ungrateful. I knew I did not want to handicap my children early in life by catering to them their material wants or making their life too easy. I would take them to Mexico every year, but they would have to help earn the money for the trip with jobs. I emphasized that even though they helped earn the money for the trip, it was a privilege to get to go to Mexico every year, not a right.

They needed to understand that life does have winners and losers, and I wanted to help them reach a level of understanding on how to regulate disappointment, as well as how to temper success. They also had to learn that gossip, ugliness, and meanness are going to be present throughout their life. If they wanted to be successful, they needed to understand this.

When my children blamed others for something they were at fault for, I taught them to have the courage to accept the blame themselves. A child who never accepts blame or is disrespectful will never have true respect for anyone. You cannot force a child to be respectful, but you can choose not to be disrespected.

I used these lessons in a practical manner by letting them earn money for completing chores in our home – including the care, landscaping, and planting of the yard. They also took on extra jobs. They helped me with my antique business, and Andrew sold newspapers, which taught him his entrepreneurial skills. All three girls babysat neighborhood children. All four would walk the neighbor's dogs as well. Andrew learned carpentry from a neighborhood carpenter, and still uses those skills today.

It is important that children realize they should start at the bottom and work their way up. I had an example for them on what not to do from another family. The parents raised their children to start out at the top, and none are successful. In fact, all but one of them became alcoholics. I never shied away from hard lessons or reality when trying to teach my children about life.

One time a client had an alcoholic son, who needed to sell his home. It was in dire need of a cleaning. There was vomit and feces everywhere, as well as empty liquor bottles hidden everywhere. He was too sick from alcoholism to clean. I decided to have Andrew go with me to the home to help clean (he wore gloves and a mask) – he earned a little bit of money and saw firsthand the danger of becoming dependent on alcohol, and how it could destroy your life. The father was very grateful that we were able to clean the home, and have it sold, and Andrew learned a valuable lesson.

I taught my children that the only way they could succeed was to always look for opportunities. They grew up in a diverse neighborhood, so they were exposed to all types of demographics. I wanted them to learn the value of hard work and self-reliance, so one summer when they were being lazy and entitled, and begged me to send them to a posh summer camp with all their friends, I said no. This did not seem like a good idea to me – to pay someone else to make them "live like kings" and become even more entitled. So, I sent them to the farm of someone I knew in Iowa for the summer. They would wake up early there and pull weeds until it became too hot to work. When parents fear their children's reactions and cater to their unreasonable demands, the future is negated for everyone. I wanted to teach them that life is not always easy, and hard work and determination pay off and help you succeed. After that experience, they became more appreciative of what they had, less entitled, and often talked of how hardworking the people of Iowa were.

I always pointed out certain destructive behaviors of others, hoping my children learned to not make similar mistakes in their future. When I saw teenagers that were tattooed, or with piercings, I always pointed out how destructive that behavior was because it kept them from future success. It drove me crazy when parents would stop parenting, and let their children do whatever they wanted. I always taught them to look people in the eye when first introduced and be polite. It made them stand out more than the lazy kids who didn't even get off the couch to greet someone. I always remembered that the teenage years were the years that a parent had to be extra careful to continue to parent. These times are critical, and a parent has to remember their children are not "their friends".

When *the Prince* disrespected me in front of the children, it served as "permission" for the children to disrespect me as well. This was always an uphill battle for me to overcome. If you have never been hated by your children, you have never been a parent.

 Conversely, I always pointed out the people who entered their lives with good values and tried to teach them to implement good values in their lives. We always ate dinner together, a practice that is sadly no longer done in many homes.

 I did not let them get away with being lazy. My kids and clients seemed to know when I was relaxing, so I showed them how not to be lazy. An example of how to be lazy presented itself when I would ask *The Prince* to put away his clothes. I had done the washing/drying/folding, but he would just never put away his clothes, and would leave his dirty socks and underwear lying around. I had started taking an upholstery class – and after years of *The Prince* never putting his socks and underwear away, I used upholstery nails to secure them to the floor. My children learned from this and would put their clothes away.

 I tried new things to keep our family healthy and happy. Being a parent means sometimes being inconvenienced. We attended family therapy, and EST. I also had to pay out of my own pocket for these sessions, but I felt it was needed. I liked to give my children jobs, activities, projects, and tasks to complete because it always helped their self-esteem when completed.

 My children always participated in the 4th of July parade in Aspen. I made them old-fashioned costumes (bonnets and all!) and they walked with a vintage pony cart. This helped their self-esteem as well and taught them not to fear "the world". This helped them participate in a fun way. I wanted to do this because when I first met Maura, she feared everything.

 Even though it is a hard subject, I taught them not to lend money to friends. That is what banks are for. If someone has the nerve to ask for a loan from a friend, they have the nerve to not pay it back. I had made this mistake multiple times in my life, so was happy to share my experiences and knowledge with my children, so they did not make the same mistakes.

 Show through example how you should treat people. Also, teach how to negotiate and be a peacemaker. Every family benefits from one. Michelle was our family's peacemaker – her positive disposition always helped the process.

 Learning these lessons were hard when they came from someone who treated people poorly. I was surprised that my synagogue was a place where one of my children learned a hard lesson on how not to treat someone. It was Maura. She had recently started Hebrew school at Temple Emanuel, and a classmate was to be Bat Mitzvah 'ed. The parent of the child invited every person in the class except Maura. It was devastating to her. I spoke with the mother and the Rabbi, and both just said, "They can invite whomever they wish." I did explain to the Rabbi that is true UNLESS you invite the entire class – then it is just exclusionary. Even the extreme kindness of the teachers, Mrs. Levy and Edie Kay, was not enough to stem the damage. After that happened, Maura started acting out at school, and to this day wants nothing to do with religion. On the other end, an Orthodox Jewish family in Denver, the Binstocks, treated our whole family with nothing but kindness, inviting us over for holidays, and welcoming us into their large family. This helped expose my children to the most beautiful part of Judaism. Sadly, this was not enough to help Maura regain her trust in religion.

When the area soccer coach for young children (under 6) would bench children that he felt were "not good enough" to play, I decided to become a coach. Sports at that age should never be exclusionary and should teach children how to play a sport or game, the rules, about teamwork, and give them a place to exercise. At a later age, benching them is fine – children need to understand that sports and games have winners and losers, just like life.

A great way I kept my children busy was to give them projects. One summer Andrew and his five friends – all eleven years old - built their clubhouse all by themselves in Aspen. The rules were that they had to find material in construction dumpsters – we would not purchase the materials for them. No one liked to use the saw, so they picked boards that (sort-of) already fit together. They learned that even if they felt discouraged, not to quit. They had to create their own floor plan – which included a trap door in the roof. Jake Glaser, one of the boys involved, says that to this day it was one of the best memories of his life.

I would take my children to the Salvation Army every Christmas, and we would bring presents and help with the Christmas meal. I was hopeful that this would help them see how to be a good citizen, and how to

Andrew's clubhouse, 1996

treat others with kindness, and respect. Like everything in life, I tried to temper the bad with the good – both are present and help children learn how to navigate their lives.

When people treat you or your children poorly, use it to teach them to do better in their own treatment of people. We had just moved into a new neighborhood, and Andrew had met the children, and played with them. A neighbor named Greta, who also happened to be a pediatric neuropsychologist at Children's Hospital, had a birthday party for all the neighborhood children, and did not invite Andrew. Andrew was five years old, and when he asked her why he wasn't invited, she stated, "She did not have enough ice cream to go around." He then came home and told me he thought his friend's mom had lied to him. I had always taught my children not to lie. He grabbed my hand and took me across the street to talk to her – he knocked on her door. When she answered, he asked her to tell me why she said he was unable to attend the neighborhood party. She immediately answered, "I do not have enough ice cream to go around." Andrew buried his head on my hip and cried. This did not move her. I found it quite troubling that a "professional" who was tasked with the care of children's emotions showed so little care of my son's. Of course, when I offered to purchase ice cream, she had no answer. The display of unkindness, and the lie was a lot for me to handle as a new neighbor, I can only imagine how hard it was for Andrew, who was only 5 at the time.

That was one of the incidents that helped manifest Andrew's low self-esteem issues he suffered throughout his childhood.

Because *The Prince* had basically taken my children's future from them during the divorce, I tried to find a way to replace the money and property that the court awarded to him (and that he claimed he would return to the children, and never did). Once I became a successful real estate agent, I decided that I would help purchase a home for each of my children to help with their future. I put the down payments on the homes and carried the mortgage at first. I carried the mortgage until they paid for it on their own. I was allowed to gift a certain amount to each of them yearly, so I would, and apply that gifted money to the mortgage. It was the best investment I made, and it helped the children on their path to success. They also worked to earn money to purchase their own cars, so they could get to their jobs.

**If your children are behaving badly, let them know that you understand their pain from a parent's point of view, but that does not make their bad behavior tolerable to the rest of the world.**

Make commitments and personal sacrifices to assure they have a future. I always honored my commitments and sacrifices, hoping that would teach my children personal responsibility as well. Mothers are like glue – holding everything together with no acknowledgement. I feel the extra work and attention did pay off in some ways because as adults, Maura started a prosperous Pilates business, Michelle teaches preschool and is a fabulous mother with an infectious personality and great sense of humor, Kay has had a long career in the real estate field, and Andrew is a successful entrepreneur, who still possesses the sweet nature he seemed to be born with.

Raising children can be a tough road. Once you sign on to be a mother, it is 24/7 – that's the only shift available. No matter if the resentment they carry is misplaced, try to understand. Never give up on them, if possible, but realize that sometimes you have to let go.

I have an excellent relationship with Michelle and Andrew, but I had to let Maura and Kay go in adulthood. I realized that I could never change their behavior and deep resentment of me as their mother. Even though I always encouraged and supported them and their interests and talents, always loved and cared for them, they treated me very poorly. I think they just did not realize that I did these things because I cared for them so much, not because I "had to".

Maura seemed to forget that I was the only one there for her, when no one else was. Sometimes you can try all you want to help someone, and never give up on them, and still end up the bad guy. I stopped seeking validation and support that was never there. You walk out of their lives, and you let go. You no longer allow the behavior. I finally accepted that I did my best, and tried my hardest for all my children, but I did have to let Maura and Kay go. You adjust to something unimaginable. You adjust to the now painful memories of how disregarded, criticized, and valueless you are in their lives. Even with this disappointment, all my children taught me to be strong, and how to allow myself to live an amazing and grateful life. My broken heart helped fix my vision.

Better You Should Cry Now, Then I Should Cry Later

# 9

# Inhaling Gratitude

From balloon crash to amazing life

usiness was great and I was happier than ever. I had good friends and a full life. Even while continuing my custody fight, Andrew was able to spend many weekends with me.

During the summers, we escaped to my family's Aspen property, a place where you just enjoyed the moments with each other.

Michelle had grown into a beautiful young woman. She was twenty-three, and she doted on her little brother Andrew.

As she became an adult, we spent more time together and I grew to trust and respect her. She was more than my daughter. She was my best friend and most fun confident. We shared a deep connection, sharing the same sense of humor, and could laugh at nothing for hours.

That summer, she and I decided it was time to have some fun. On the drive to Aspen, we sang silly songs with Andrew and talked about our past trips. I told them stories about Aspen before it became a resort town; how I had run wild there as a child, how Aspen children created their own fun and how the people treated us like family.

The first morning of our vacation, we woke to the roaring sound of hot-air balloons preparing to take flight. The balloons were taking off in a park within walking distance of our house and we loved to watch them launch.

Drinking coffee, Michelle and I watched the colorful balloons lifting their baskets into the blue sky. It was a gorgeous Colorado morning.

When she was younger, Michelle had dreamed of flying in one of those balloons, and I had promised her I would take us on a balloon adventure someday.

It was a splurge, but an adventure would be good for us.

I knew the owner of the small Aspen company and made a reservation for the following day, a Sunday. We were booked on a six person balloon.

That Saturday morning, Michelle, Andrew and I headed out for garage sales, excited about our big adventure the next day.

That afternoon, when we got home, there was a message that, because of a mix-up, our reservation had been given away to a family from Tennessee. I was furious, and phoned the owner, demanding our reservation be honored. She refused, saying that the family was not going to be back in Aspen, and we would. My anger at being disregarded became a lesson on tempering anger in the future when the pilot of that balloon, and all its passengers, including the family from Tennessee, died when the balloon crashed. You can only be grateful and thank the circumstances that allowed you and your children to live, while still feeling sorrow for the ones that did not. **Once again, out of everything bad that happens, something good happened. Our lives were saved.**

Determined to make our adventure happen, I called one of the larger outfits. They were happy to take us up first thing Sunday morning. It was a twelve-person balloon.

Michelle, Andrew, and I were very excited. I couldn't wait to see Aspen from the air. It would be fun to float above the evergreens, see the rushing river, and the mountain peaks.

The three of us spent the rest of Saturday in anticipation. We talked about it over dinner and went to bed early so we could rise at dawn for our big ride in the sky.

Early Sunday, we walked to the spot where our balloon was scheduled to launch at Rio Grande Park. The morning was calm and cool, though I noticed a few dark clouds in the distance.

Our pilot helped us into the basket. A group of four was already on board.

We watched another balloon taking to the sky, and had to shout to hear each other. Helpers released the tethers that held us to the ground and we floated quickly skyward. It was exciting! Andrew peered down enthusiastically at the shrinking trees and homes below us.

By the time we touched down to pick up the other passengers, the dark clouds were looming closer and the wind was picking up.

"Is it okay to fly in this?" I asked the pilot. "No big deal," she assured me.

I assumed she knew what she was doing. After all, every day during the summer these balloons flew multiple trips over Aspen.

But the weather changed quickly.

A storm blew in. The sky was menacing and the wind biting, and it started raining heavily. I felt uneasy about flying in such weather.

I heard the pilot on the radio, someone advising her to get to the ground.

The balloon that had taken off before us seemed to wobble in the sky. We watched as its fabric appeared rippled and distorted in the wind near us.

I felt our own basket shiver as the strong wind turned cold in the deep, corrugated gray sky.

The wobbly balloon ahead of us suddenly dipped and jerked upward and seemed to bend.

Then everything seemed to unfold in slow motion. We watched in horror as the balloon ahead of us crashed into power lines 20 yards west of the famous Woody Creek Tavern, severing the balloon from its basket.

The basket plummeted towards the ground, and through an opening in the cottonwoods, we saw the basket implode, it was clear there were no survivors. To our horror, the severed balloon continued to follow our balloon's flight path.

That was the balloon we were originally scheduled to fly in. Fate's way of saving my life, again. But this time, it extended to my children.

Our pilot then assured us, "That won't happen to us."

But I could see in her eyes that she didn't believe her own words.

She tried to take us down in a nearby field, but the wind caught us and dragged our basket, until I thought we were in the river instead. We were not in the river, but it seemed like it with all the water from the rain. The rain was so heavy that I thought the propane tanks may be leaking, and was worried about the balloon catching fire. The balloon completely obscured my vision. It was like driving a speeding car with the hood up. You knew you were going to hit something, but you could not see it happening.

Suddenly the wind changed, the balloon moved out of my vision, and I saw that we seemed to be on a collision course through a very large window of a home.

"Crash position!" the pilot yelled, but she hadn't prepared us for what to do.

"What's crash position?" I hollered over the strong winds. "Sit on the floor!" she screamed. "Your backs to each other!"

On the floor of the basket, we wouldn't be able to see if we were close to the ground. I had spent my whole life being blindsided. I could not sit there with my eyes closed, waiting to die, especially not with Michelle and Andrew with me. Anytime I had allowed others to make decisions for me, it had turned out badly. I decided to stay upright with the pilot.

I kept standing and braced against the wind, ready to navigate this new danger.

The balloon dipped, then soared. We skimmed the tree line and barely missed the power lines. We dipped again, lower. For a moment, it seemed we might land. But the wind caught us again and we hit a large fence.

The impact tipped us over, and the pilot tumbled out!

The rest of us rose into the sky, without a pilot. I grabbed at the rope she had been maneuvering, wrapped it around my arm for leverage and put all my weight into it.

We then descended too quickly. The bottom of our basket bumped across the rain soaked grasses of an open field. It was all we could do to hang on.

We neared the ground again and, as the basket touched down, I screamed at Michelle to jump out, and she did. I quickly grabbed Andrew and threw him out of the basket. With all the adrenaline, he seemed to weigh almost nothing.

The balloon pulled me away from them and I heard him screaming for me.

I tried to jump out, but my arm was entwined in the rope and every bounce of the balloon was throwing me off the floor of the basket like a puppet on a string.

Finally, the balloon crashed in a stretch of open field and I jumped, my arm tearing as the rope ripped from me.

Seven people were still inside the 1,500-pound basket, which struck me in the chest as it whipped around and continued to drag them away, leaving me behind, crumpled on the ground.

My arm was ripped open from the coarse rope where it had tethered me to the balloon. It gushed blood. In excruciating pain, I vomited blood and fought to breathe.

Michelle and Andrew rushed to me. He screamed for help, "My mom is dying, please help." Michelle held my head, and kept removing the blood from my mouth that I was choking on. She continued talking with me until help arrived.

An ambulance finally showed up, but emergency teams had trouble finding us in the tall, uncut field. It seemed like it took forever.

When paramedics put me in the ambulance, it was as if my whole body had broken apart. I had never experienced so much pain.

At the hospital in Aspen, my blood pressure dropped, and the doctors wouldn't give me anesthesia. They thought I may have lacerated my aorta.

They performed an emergency procedure because of my collapsed lungs. "It will hurt," I was told, but nothing could have prepared me for the agony. Tubes were inserted without anesthesia, and they opened my chest on the side to insert these tubes (I called them "garden hoses") into my chest cavity to remove the excess air and let my lungs reinflate. The Dr. stated he could not believe I stayed conscience throughout the procedure, although it did take an entire staff to hold me down. After the procedure, the doctor said I can't believe you are still here. I replied, "That was as bad as family court, but I survived that, too.

Michelle was by my side the whole time, and had to leave the room to vomit after watching them insert chest tubes into my lungs, later telling me it was the worst thing she had ever witnessed.

The doctor believed I was dying. He told Michelle, "Her chances aren't good. You should tell her everything you want to." We had a very special moment together that we still treasure today. We both said goodbye at that moment and it taught us the value of all our future moments. Michelle had outgrown my lap, but she never would outgrow my heart.

I was bleeding internally and the hospital in Aspen wasn't equipped to handle such a serious injury. I was airlifted and rushed to St. Mary's Hospital in Grand Junction. During the flight, I was finally given a morphine drip to help with the pain and was allowed to pump it at my own discretion. The morphine made me very sick. By the time we arrived at St. Mary's, I was throwing up with a crushed chest. The level of pain was beyond belief. After this experience, I refused more pain medication, even though my prognosis was poor.

Thankfully, both Michelle and Andrew were okay physically after the accident. She had injured her knees but would recover. Remarkably, Andrew was unscathed. It was like winning the lottery.

Denver Post article, August 1993

I realized how lucky my family was. That easily could have been us in the first balloon. Even through my intense pain and the fog of the medication, I was grateful. We weren't meant to be in that particular balloon. That wasn't our fate that day. We had survived.

Six people died that day, eleven more were treated for injuries. At the time, it was the worst hot air balloon crash in the history of the United States, and one of the worst in the world. Balloon crashes are rare, and they are almost always tragic.

My Aspen neighbor, Paula Mayer, picked up Andrew and looked after him until someone could reach his father. Michelle stayed with me.

News of the crash was on the front page of The Denver Post. Under the headline "Six People Killed in Aspen Balloon Accident," they used a photo of Andrew and me. Anyone who looked at the headlines, and did not read the entire article would assume we were dead.

My brother and his wife drove all the way to Grand Junction. I thought they had come to visit me. I was wrong. Instead, they presented me with a legal document their lawyer had created, wanting me to sign over my share of a family property in Aspen before I died.

I might have been physically broken, but I certainly was not mentally broken. I was shocked that they chose to take advantage of my vulnerability at this time to try and get me to sign documents allowing them to sell my Aspen property. I said, "No."

I continued my recovery in intensive care at St. Mary's until I was served canned peaches in August. That was all the incentive I needed to leave the hospital. Palisade Colorado is near Grand Junction, and is the peach capital of Colorado. I could have gone outside and picked a fresh peach.

It was time. I had a business to run.

After all, there are hospitals in Denver. Michelle took an eggshell mattress from the hospital, put it in the car, and drove me to Denver. I was transferred to St. Joseph's Hospital in Denver. The doctor came outside, since I could not get out of the car on my own. She stated that after evaluating my x-rays, she was going to admit me to the ICU, and put chest tubes to drain the fluids from my lungs. I informed her this was never going to happen. She kept insisting, and told me my insurance would be canceled if I did not follow her instructions. I told her I would never again have chest tubes. I also said losing Kaiser insurance was no big loss. I then asked her if she knew why Jesus was born in a manger, and told her it was because his parents had Kaiser Insurance.

I then defiantly said, "I haven't seen the roots of my hair since I was sixteen. I have a hair appointment at four o'clock at my house with my friend and hairdresser, Linda Pascoe." I didn't mention that my nails were in need of hedge clippers.

To solve the problem, I had Michelle contact a pulmonologist friend who worked in a building next to the hospital, and she pushed me in my wheelchair over to see him. While in his office, he wrote me a prescription to have my hair done. He knew my humor, and realized it would help my spirit.

He then performed a procedure to empty my lungs of the remaining fluid, it was such a relief to be able to breathe, and also to realize my hair was getting done. I went home. It felt wonderful to be there, even though I was immediately presented with legal papers and a lawsuit from my brother. He still wanted a decision on the Aspen property, even though I had been fighting for my life. He did this to me at my most vulnerable moment. To avoid court, I settled by paying him a large sum of money to buy him out and become the sole owner of the property.

I was still very sick and had a lot of recovering to do, but I knew I would never get well in a hospital. Hospitals and doctors brought back too many terrible memories. I might go through years of treatment and pain, but I was determined to live in my own home. I was ready to get back to work. I had to.

My divorce agreement required me to pay a very large sum of money to *The Prince* each month. Plus, I had my own expenses, including new medical bills piling up. Insurance covered some of the treatments but not all. The hospital in Grand Junction was out of my network and I had to cover those bills out of pocket.

Promotion after balloon accident

It was a constant struggle dealing with the physical injuries and arguing with the insurance company about paying for treatments at the same time. That was a full time job on top of the full time job I already had in real estate.

After the newspaper headlines, plenty of people I had worked with through the years assumed I was dead or nearly so, and most of them could not believe how quickly I returned to work. It would take more than a balloon crash to stop me.

As I always had, I tried to make the best of my situation. I printed up ads with a picture of a hot air balloon and the message: "Still selling!" I got a ton of phone calls after that. No one could believe I would make a joke about something that had nearly killed me. They didn't know how many times I had been that close to death before.

It was important to me not to lose clients because of the crash. I also didn't want to lose my sense of humor. Even so, the repercussions of the crash were real and long term. It took me more than ten years to feel whole again. Because of my chest injuries, my diaphragm and esophagus were compromised, which made breathing difficult. I could no longer sleep on my back. I had to prop myself up on a pile of pillows to keep from choking, and I had great difficulty keeping any food down. My painful, hacking cough persisted for years.

The company that had operated the balloon tried to declare the crash as an unavoidable accident. They offered me a $5,000 settlement if I would sign away my rights to sue. Of course, I didn't take it.

My medical bills were crippling. I then learned that other balloon companies had chosen not to launch that morning because the weather reports had warned of possible wind shear and rain. When I had booked the trip, I'd considered it a fun excursion, never contemplating that it could have life changing consequences. Now I realized how serious it was to board a hot air balloon. **We should have received information about what to do in the event of a crash landing. We should have been trained in the safety procedures and precautions.** The company didn't do any of this. They didn't want to scare off their customers.

I sued, as did several of the other passengers. My injuries were the most severe, so my case dragged on the longest. The evidence was overwhelmingly on my side. The balloon never should have launched that morning. The pilot should have aborted the flight before we took off. She had ignored the weather warnings as well as the advice to get down to the ground.

The balloon company tried to blame me for my injuries, saying I had refused to sit down. But I knew that sitting down would not have kept us from crashing, and so did anyone who looked at the reports. In the deposition in court, the lawyer asked me why I didn't follow instructions to "Get in to crash position." I replied that I was never properly briefed on this, and I wanted to see how we were going to die…. that my children needed protection, and I was not the type of mother to sit in the bottom of a basket and wait for us to die.

One of the men in our basket had filmed most of the flight, so we had visual proof of the sky darkening and everything that happened. He even captured the crash of the balloon ahead of us where all the people were killed. It was horrific to watch it again.

The hearings dragged on and on. It was almost like being back in my divorce proceedings. I hated the court experiences. All I wanted was enough to cover my medical bills and some assurance that regulations would be put in place to prevent serious incidents/accidents from happening in the future. **I wanted better instructions for passengers. I wanted them to stop treating a balloon ride like a carnival ride.**

I wasn't in it for money. I wanted to make the industry safer. Ultimately, we settled rather than going to trial. This was disappointing because it meant the company wouldn't be subjected to public scrutiny for its negligence.

However, I couldn't bear the idea of sitting in a courtroom again, where attorneys often lied and made the victim responsible and where judges often ignored facts. I knew the lawyers were trying to make it seem like I was responsible. After working with attorneys to fight the nanny service and throughout my divorce, I had learned that most lawyers weren't willing to do the necessary work to go to trial.

I hired a Denver lawyer with a reputation for being a shark, but the outcome was disheartening. I fought as long and hard as I could.

By the time we reached a settlement, it had almost been three years since the balloon crash. I was still in pain, and had to sleep in an upright position because of my lung injuries. I often cleared rooms with my deep cough. Michelle and Andrew were both struggling emotionally with what they experienced that day. I did everything I could to help them heal. I was so grateful they had survived the crash with few physical injuries.

Right after the balloon crash, *The Prince* filed another brief with the courts, claiming I was not fit to care for Andrew, even occasionally, claiming it was reckless to take a child up in a balloon.

I didn't see Andrew again for two more months because of his actions. It took six months for the courts to reinstate the previous agreement, and for Andrew to stay with me again. It was like my brother and *the Prince* were joining forces to "Trip a Cripple."

Yet I did not break down, give up, or give in.

Michelle, Andrew and I survived. That was all that mattered.

I made the choice at that time to step away from the court system. I had wanted to hold the balloon company accountable to their future passengers, by forcing them to train and provide safety measures to all passengers, in the event they were ever in a crash situation, or needed to fly the balloon if the pilot became incapacitated. I also believed the inherent dangers of balloon rides should have been disclosed, and the passengers should have had a chance to review, and sign. The low amount of insurance carried ($5000 total on a 12-man balloon) was ridiculous. After standing my ground to (at least) hold the balloon company responsible for my medical bills, I decided to shut the book on it, since I no longer had the stomach to participate in the sewer that engulfs the legal system. **You can not soar if you let people and events destroy your flight.**

# 10

# Putting the Pieces of the Puzzle Together

Women's Support Groups

The terms of my divorce decree were so unexpected, and unfathomable, I felt a sense of being lost in a sudden, harsh storm. With Andrew and Kay gone from my home, I had a hard time getting out of bed. To have them taken from me was terrible for all of us. I saw it in their eyes whenever they visited. Kay stopped coming to see me, and she never lived in my home again - although I did still pay for everything for her, even when her father abandoned her. Those were very dark days. What I felt was beyond words. I shut down my feelings and compartmentalized my sadness, shock, and defeat. **Strength isn't always shown in what you can hold on to, sometimes it's shown in what you had to let go of.** I would not go see a therapist, though I knew I was depressed. After my experiences, I did not trust any of them. I did allow myself to mourn for a while, but I soon got back to work. I had to get my feet back under me, and learn to laugh again. The divorce had stripped me of everything I had earned. But it was more than that. Work was a lifeboat. I turned to it for my sense of fulfillment and the recovery of my identity. Work was the one place I felt valued and competent.

I began to wake up to the possibilities of my new situation. Business was booming and I loved going to work. I no longer needed to rise at 4am to do housework, or stay up half the night working on marketing materials. I could stay at the office if I needed to. I was rebuilding my life. It was a new future to create. I began to think about getting Andrew back. At least joint custody. I knew he needed me.

Everything I had done in my life had been a defense mechanism, to protect myself as much as I was projecting an image to the world. I'd thought I was doing the right thing. I believed, if I pretended, I was happy, I would be happy. If I pretended to love my husband, maybe I could learn to love him. Maybe he would love me. Even my imagination was not that good.

After our divorce, I learned for the first time to enjoy life. I knew any energy spent trying to get revenge would be better spent creating a new, amazing life. **Life is a choice made by you alone.** That is the only way I found my way out.

The next year I figured that my assistant Jeannie, my daughter Michelle and I needed relief from life's dramas. I was coming to terms with my losses, Michelle was adjusting to being removed from her senior year of college due to the court ruling on the amount of money I had to pay *the Prince*, which did not leave enough for her tuition, and Jeannie was recovering from the tragedy of her father going to prison for shooting her mother and three sisters (luckily, they all survived). We decided to go to Mexico. While we were on the beach in Playa del Carmen, laying on our beach chairs, a naked man strolled up and introduced himself as Peter from Switzerland. He acted like being naked was no big deal, so Jeannie, Michelle and I burst out laughing, until the "tears" ran down our legs. We never resumed our composure. It was just what we needed – laughter and fun.

We soon discovered that our wonderful beach resort was next to a nudist beach, which just increased the fun. We went back year after year

Denice, Michelle and Jeannie in Mexico

The beautiful beach front before over-development

with our families and friends. These moments kept me going. We had such a great time, and I returned to Playa del Carmen every December, forming friendships with the people who did the same. We called them our "December Families." Twenty-five years after I had first gone there, the hotel was sold to a Texas group. We were all devastated because we thought it was sold to a big hotel chain, and our little grass huts on the beach would be replaced with a huge concrete hotel. Luckily that did not happen, and the only change the new owners wanted was to change the name. The hotel had been called Shangrila, and the new owners wanted to change the name. They invited us to give suggestions to rename the hotel. We said, "This place is magical, and they ended up naming it Mahekal (a take on the Spanish word for magical – majico).

Each of us told our stories of why we loved the hotel. I told of what had happened years before when my grandchildren were playing with another set of grandchildren. Everyone always talked with each other. I found out that this family's grandfather introduced non- rustable (stainless steel) from Sweden to America. Years later, the grandfather convinced Walter Chrysler to use this non-rustable (stainless steel) for the roof on the Chrysler building in the late 1920s. He also introduced the Mayo Brothers to the non-rustable (stainless steel) application for surgical instruments and convinced them to use them, he also convinced Dr. Lillehei to use these stainless-steel surgical instruments in his practice. As soon as I heard the name, I told him, "What a small world."

The little girl playing with your grandchildren, Lilly, was named after his grandson, Dr. Kevin Lillehei – a famous neurosurgeon in Denver who removed a brain tumor on my daughter, Michelle. It was always our December place of discovery, laughter, and shared friendships, where you forget the world and just enjoyed the moment.

Jeannie knew how difficult the divorce and custody battle had been for me. When the divorce was nearly final, she came up with the idea of a divorce party. "You need to do something big and momentous to celebrate your freedom," she said. She is one of those friends who make you laugh, even when you think you'll never smile again. She once told me, "You cuss too much, you're everything I ever wanted in a friend."

We invited several friends, including the realtor Chaz Averson, who'd given Jeannie a place to stay when she first came to Denver. This wonderful, funny man showed up in drag, wearing an old bride's dress from Goodwill. He'd torn it to shreds and had rolled around in the dirt, so he looked a mess.

"It's symbolic," he said, "because you've been dragged through the mud."

We had a big cake, like a wedding cake but with icing and black roses. There were "adult versions" of many children's games like Pin the Tail on the Donkey that used obscene images of *The Prince's* face which appeared time and time again in rather unusual places. There was toilet paper that had his photo on it and too many other lewd incidentals to mention. It was silly, uproarious and so inappropriate but I wanted to create new memories of fun and laughter. Knowing I'd respond better to humor than to a day at a spa, it was exactly what I needed. I had the best friends.

We were all but done with the years of bitter court hearings. The party was an immense relief, and a symbolic way to put the past behind me. Life is about the good, the bad, and the ugly.

Around this time, the Kemp Center called me to list the Olinger Mortuary house. I asked, "Why did you pick me?"

They told me it was because of my work trying to improve childcare.

Marilyn Van Derbur, one of the heirs to the Olinger Mortuaries was the person I met with while listing the house. Meeting her profoundly changed the rest of my life. A former Miss America, Marilyn had been sexually abused in her childhood by her father.

She'd written a book, *Miss America By Day,* and was speaking out publicly about what it was like to recover after years of abuse at the hands of someone you trust as a child.

Marilyn had started a program called Survivors United Network (SUN). I joined the first class of 50, confused as to why I was even there.

Gretchen Broiler Hagerman worked for SUN and put classes together for women who were survivors. She was a genius. She put us in circles of ten, and asked each of us to stand up if we had been sexually abused by a father, a brother, uncle, or babysitter, etc.

After everyone had stood, except for me and two others, she then said to us, "Were any of you ever abused by your mother?" One of the remaining three stood. I did not. I felt embarrassed that I was even there.

Then Gretchen described how mothers can abuse their children sexually. I realized she was describing what happened to me, and I stood up, as did the remaining sitting participant.

**She taught us about understanding our own behavior, and how our memories trigger us – to suicide, cutting, anorexia, and other eating disorders, or become perfectionists, etc.** She then had everyone retake their seats. She asked each of us to stand up if we had ever tried to commit suicide, had cut ourselves, had an eating disorder, etc. Soon everyone was standing again.

**I attended and learned how my past had impacted my choices. That insight gave me the ability to make better choices and change my behaviors. I learned to accept the shame I had lived with all my life and to accept the intense need for perfection I had carried with me. I learned so much from the other survivors and through Gretchen.**

My defiant personality was my protection. I often express myself in outrageous or inappropriate, conversation killing ways. For example, I swear a lot – even though my mother "washed" my mouth out with cayenne pepper. I keep doing it as almost a badge of survival, although I know it is self-destructive. **I delight in being outrageous while expressing myself even though I know it is destructive, because of the lasting effects of the shocking sexual abuse I suffered in my childhood.**

Like many, I had always thought my childhood was normal. It was healing to learn that it wasn't. I learned why I had made the choices I made since then, and the coping mechanisms I had developed during the broken trust of my early childhood.

I learned that my suicide attempt driving my car at 16 was a coping mechanism triggered by my childhood shame, that I carried from my mother and brother. **I learned why I had continued to attract so much betrayal into my life.** I had been reliving my past ingrained reactions, even while hoping each new event would turn out differently. I had continued to pick abusive relationships. I began to understand how my past influenced my future choices.

I began to see the truth of my learned responses and choices. I learned that every survivor of abuse feels this way, and that this is part of what gives the perpetrator so much power. They revel in making us feel weak and culpable.

They want us to take the blame, and often threaten to tell others that we willingly participated in their abuse. As if somehow, that lets them off the hook. After I realized that, I began to feel the repressed memories of my brother. **Guilt is feeling bad about what you have done, shame is feeling bad about who you are.**

Putting all the pieces together was a challenge, because most of the pieces were difficult or missing. It all came together after SUN, piece by piece.

I never forgave the abusers, but I forgave myself, and was able to forget them. I was not alone. In fact, the number of women like me were overwhelming. Our silence was a global phenomenon. Many studies have been conducted, and some put the number of women abused in childhood as high as 25%

**After the shame I had carried my whole life, it was a relief to forgive myself, and understand I was a survivor, and recognize how destructive my coping mechanisms had been.** I learned that avoiding certain people was healthy, not a weakness. It was like one of the main pieces of a puzzle was set in place. At 48 years old, I was a complex human being who had built a life for myself despite the odds.

I am grateful to Marilyn for her immense courage and commitment to educate fellow survivors. Someone once asked me, "Why are you called survivors?" I replied, "Because most have survived suicide attempts."

**Whenever you find yourself doubting how far you can go, just remember how far you have come.**

Life is like a puzzle. Every piece fits together to create who we become.

If someone asked after all that happened in my life what has been the most difficult, my answer would be immediate: the divorce court where "motherhood" was on trial. All my years spent working, only wanting the best for my children, was on trial. The psychiatrist, judges, psychologist, custody evaluators, lawyers, had no understanding of adoption, teenagers, epilepsy or the immense stress of being the primary money earner. Instead of emphasizing what I did right as a mother, the court chose to focus instead on what the opposing criminal attorney felt I did wrong. He was a master at creating a smoke screen. Using my decades old medical history to further his case, and never acknowledging the multiplicity of roles I had dealt with for over twenty years – a task overload on a daily basis. All my efforts over the years to make sure they went to the best schools – even driving 88 miles/day for six years, that they had orthodontic work, that they were able to participate in all their extracurricular activities, etc….were dismissed by the courts. All these efforts, and all our precious memories were ignored in the expert's desire to only portray me in a negative light. In spite of this, I was determined to live a happy life. They assassinated my character, but they could not kill my intentions to be the best I could possibly be.

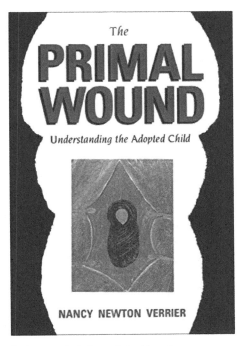

The
# PRIMAL WOUND
Understanding the Adopted Child

NANCY NEWTON VERRIER

Book every adopted parent should read

After the court case was over, I found a class on adoption. **Once again, I discovered that out of everything bad comes an opportunity for good.** Liz Clarke was the incredible teacher who introduced Nancy Verrier's book *Primal Wound: Understanding the Adopted Child.* My huge takeaway was and is today: You cannot fix adopted children. The deep resentment these children often carry with them toward the adopting mother is immense. The rejection by the birth mother, no matter the reason, is a void in their lives that is always there. **The target for resentment becomes and remains the adoptive mother.** Sometimes you can try as hard as you can to help a child, and never give up on them, and still you end up as the "bad guy."

You can only give them the tools to be productive citizens. Verrier's book was such a validation of all the heartbreak I had experienced.

I learned that many adopted children have huge problems with learning in school. When Kay, Maura and Andrew were growing up, I thought I was just a bad mother—that the private schools for learning disabilities would resolve their issues. At that time, there were no books on the studies of adoption. In fact, the belief was that adoption was a wonderful solution to everyone involved and all would live happily ever after. This is not always true. **If you have never been hated by your child, you have never been a parent.**

For me, my focus was to get my kids the best education possible for their needs, and to love them.

It was a very questioning time to raise children I loved with all my heart and soul. Yet each of them in their own way was incapable of attachment. Maura was the family saboteur, having temper tantrums, and acting out- ruining every joyful family moment, and mean-spirited manipulating everything she could as she matured. These actions were fueled by her feelings of abandonment from both her birth mother and *the Prince.* Kay was not subtle in her actions. She was always angry, expressing often: "You are not my real mother." Some children cause happiness wherever they go, others whenever they go. Sometimes the children you take bullets for end up being the ones behind the gun.

I felt a draining sense of failure on a daily basis. She was one of those people at war with themselves, and I learned that she needed to cause destruction and chaos to get attention. People at war with themselves will always cause destruction in the lives around them. You can not control them, you just have to accept them for what they are, and move on, excluding them from your life. I tried my hardest, yet no matter what I did, no matter how hard I tried, I ultimately realized I was of no value to her. I finally found the courage to let her go and live her life in the confines of her self destructive system.

Andrew was different. He struggled in every way possible to be liked by everyone. He was always very affectionate, and we were great pals. He had an almost uncanny sense of entrepreneurship. When he was twelve, and for the next three years, I took him to Zig Ziglar's Power Talks, where he met Gorbachev, Giulliani, and other powerful people to keep him motivated. He was the youngest participant, and people were very impressed with his enthusiasm. The organizers even gave him a ticket to attend the event, "How to Protect your Future Finances." After attending this event, he let me know that I should set up a Family Limited Partnership for the family. It was one of the best pieces of advice I had received at the time. Although he still struggled in school, he has excelled in life. He makes my heart smile, and we still talk every day.

Denice and Andrew, 1999

I learned about the journey of adoption.

Before you accept the baby into your heart, you should do some research. In reading the book *Primal Wound,* I learned to accept the outcome of adoption. Andrew did come back to me, and calls me daily, yet my heart goes out to Maura and Kay, and I am forever sorry I cannot heal the void they carry. I gave them extra time and attention, but it never seemed to help. I spent so much time that Michelle actually said to me when she was five, "Mom, can I be adopted, too?" As the years went by, I finally realized that I could never fix their deep resentment, they had no acknowledgement of gratitude, just a self-destructive wound not capable of healing. I let them go with deep love and no longer have the capacity to deal with the cruelness that is a part of their behavior toward me.

**I learned that if the past calls, you don't answer. It has nothing new to say.** You will know you are completely done with someone when you give them up, and feel freedom instead of loss. It took half of my adult life to fit the pieces of this particular puzzle together. It was the adoption group that helped me understand the bigger picture, that is adoption. I always questioned why Maura and Kay were so unsupportive compared to Andrew, who was also adopted (through surrogacy), when they were raised in the same environment. I decided it was a matter of choice. Their choice was to be angry and resentful, while his was to accept that Claudia was his birth mother, and I was his mom.

Putting all the pieces together was my biggest challenge. I sought out, and was lucky enough to find women's support groups with members that had similar experiences. This was so empowering and comforting because instead of just psychologists/psychiatrists with theories and no practical experience, I finally understood that I was not alone. Think of it as going to a male OBGYN – he can tell you what he thinks you feel, but he does not have the experience of those feelings himself. **It can never be authentic, and neither are the psychologists/psychiatrists and their theories.** I still meet once a month with the adoption group, and their personal journeys, deep pain, and the laughter they share that are all part of having adopted children has helped me put the missing pieces together in my life. The puzzle is the journey of life that teaches you about the pieces that fit through group input, and never picking up the pieces that don't fit. **I learned that when you try to fit the wrong piece of the puzzle in your life, then nothing moves. I learned to trust my instincts, and do the unexpected instead. I was no longer stuck in that painful place where I did not belong. For me, my broken heart fixed my vision.** When you start recognizing your worth, you no longer stay around people who don't. I could not forget my past (or forgive myself) until I understood it. **Healing didn't mean the damage never existed for me, it meant it no longer controlled my life. When I let go of the damage it was an immense feeling of freedom.**

# 11

# If It Is Meant to Be, It Is up to Me

Only Dead Fish Go with the Flow

Complaining only makes you feel like a victim. Creating a new outcome with hard work empowers you to create a better result for your life. In the middle of difficulty lies a lot of opportunities. I have been presented with many opportunities to change things for the better. Depending on the timing, confidence level, and necessity, I always spoke out against the defects that needed to change. I had a voice, and it gave me the strength to speak out. It was never easy to do this against the accepted norms or opinions. Often these were unacceptable because of misinformation, and "expert's" opinions. For instance, putting epileptics in an asylum. People needed to be educated, yet I was too young and lacking self-esteem to fight that battle, so I never spoke of it. When I worked for Pan Am, I understood why they wanted someone with a good appearance and had surgery to accommodate that belief. There was an accepted elegance that defined PanAm, and I did what it took to secure the job.

I filed MedWatch reports with the FDA, hoping to recall the Bausch & Lomb Crystalens/Trulign (intraocular) lens since they have had thousands of very serious complaints about severe complications, including blindness. I have been dealing with the repercussions of having one implanted since 2016. The FDA refused to do anything, saying the "Statute of Limitations" was over, but I continue to help others who are fighting this defective implant.

I chose not to complain, but to use my ability to bring to light these injustices and try to fix them. I am the proudest of our nanny house bill, which we fought to enact through the state legislature. It was appalling for me to realize that children can be killed or injured because our society was not willing to accept that women worked outside the home, and not willing to pay a higher salary for daycare, or for background checks. This bill, which became law stops not only previous abusers, but pedophiles as well. We also educated the public through this bill's platform on the dangers of shaking a child.

I was appointed to the governor's task force on childcare. It was mainly political appointments on this task force, and I was the only member who had experienced an injured child from a caregiver. Because of this, I had to try and educate the other members on the issues involved. **It is always frustrating to try and have someone hear you, and understand the realities of a problem, when their opinions make them deaf to the facts.**

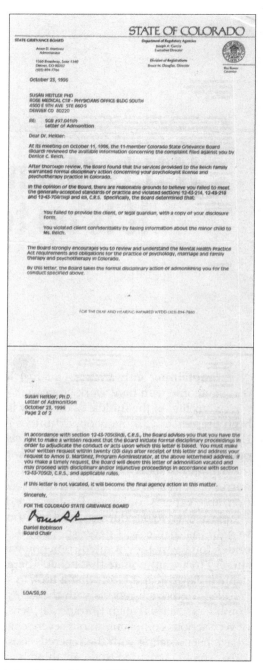

Letter of admonishment, 1996

It It Is Meant to Be, It Is up to Me

BOARD OF MEDICAL EXAMINERS
Susan Miller
Program Administrator

1560 Broadway, Suite 1300
Denver, CO 80202-5140
(303) 894-7690

Department of Regulatory Agencies
Joseph A. Garcia
Executive Director

Division of Registrations
Bruce W. Douglas, Director

LETTER OF ADMONITION

Case No. 5196010480

Marita J. Keeling, M.D.
4495 Hale Parkway, Suite 310
Denver, CO 80220

Dear Dr. Keeling:

Inquiry Panel A of the Colorado Board of Medical Examiners hereby administers disciplinary action to you in the form of this letter of admonition. Based upon Board records, the Panel finds:

In 1984, you began a physician/patient relationship with patient A, then a 32-year-old male. You treated patient A regularly for the next five years. During the course of treatment, you diagnosed Post Traumatic Stress Disorder as the primary diagnosis. Patient A received individual and group therapy from you, both of which ended on 08/30/89.

Approximately one year after you began treating Patient A, you began a physician/patient relationship with patient B, patient A's wife. At various times, over the next four years, you provided individual and group therapy to patient B. You also provided marital therapy to A and B. B's therapy ended on 09/06/89.

While A and B were receiving therapy in 1989, you perceived that they gained therapeutic benefit from their commitment and involvement in their religion. You felt that you could also benefit professionally from a similar religious experience. In May 1989, you and B accompanied A to church where he gave a private confession. During the spring and summer of 1989, A and/or B invited you to join them in church activities. At that time, you stated to B that your role as therapist could not be resumed once you changed roles to a friend and attended religious programs with them. Nevertheless, at about the time of termination of therapy, you became involved in church activities with A and B. It is the Panel's opinion that your involvement in these activities constituted a boundary violation.

In August, 1989, while still in a therapeutic relationship with A and B, you attended a hypnosis conference in California. A and B also attended that conference. After dinner one evening, you and A went for a walk along the beach, without B.

FOR THE DEAF AND HEARING IMPAIRED: V/TDD (303) 894-7880

EXHIBIT
B

becoming effective, this Order shall be open to on and shall be reported as required by law.

_____
Respondent

4495 Hale Phwy # 310
_____
Denver CO 80220
Address

AND SWORN to before me in the County of
State of Colorado, this 26 day of
199 8.

_____
NOTARY PUBLIC

LINDA J. HENRY
NOTARY

My Commission expires:
_____ 2000

It is the Panel's opinion that the boundary violations outlined above interfered with an appropriate treatment termination by you with either A or B, and your planned transition from a doctor-patient relationship to a friend relationship was not appropriate due to significant transference and countertransference problems.

After "official" termination of the therapeutic relationship with patients A and B, your relationship with A and B intensified. You were a frequent visitor in A and B's home. You converted to A and B's religion. You joined their church, bible study group and church bowling league. On one occasion, you and A went to a shooting range. It is the Panel's opinion that your subsequent personal relationship with A and B continued to be a boundary violation due to the lack of appropriate termination of the therapeutic relationship.

The Panel finds that you inappropriately crossed boundaries in your relationship with these patients, in ways that fall below generally accepted standards of medical practice for psychiatrists in violation of § 12-36-117(1)(p), C.R.S. (1991).

The Panel hereby admonishes you and cautions you that complaints disclosing any repetition of such conduct may lead to the commencement of formal disciplinary proceedings against your license to practice medicine, wherein this letter of admonition may be entered into as evidence of aggravation.

Very truly yours,

FOR THE BOARD OF MEDICAL EXAMINERS
INQUIRY PANEL A

Irene Aguilar, M.D.
Chair

Keeling letter of admonition

I spoke out about domestic violence, and the judge who claimed women that were successful could not be victims of domestic abuse. I chose to try and educate women on the myths of custody evaluators, and the gross unfairness of family court. I also wanted to bring to light that the psychiatrist(s)/psychologist(s) you think are there to listen and help you, may just be gathering ammunition to use in court against you. What needs to be understood is that every "professional" involved in the process does not have any accepted industry ethical standards. They share anything that is discussed with them, and they frequently make up diagnoses to fit their narrative. This was not disclosed.

These self-righteous predictions consumed them, and they never tried to find the truth. Later, I went against these "professionals", who had betrayed me and my trust, and was able to have the state board issue "letters of admonishment" to hold them accountable for their actions. One of these "professional's" lies about me were beyond belief. I was never her patient, yet she "diagnosed" me. The result? My complaint landed her in front of the State Grievance Board. She received a letter of admonishment as well, which became a public record on July 18th, 1997. These professionals were once protected expert witnesses, but a letter of admonishment makes them unable to testify as an expert witness again unless they acknowledge they had been censured, which makes it difficult for them be hired by the court system.

One of the professionals that had been admonished by the State Board of Medical Examiners, a psychiatrist, is no longer licensed in the state of Colorado. I continued to fight this unjust system, and was finally awarded joint custody of Andrew when he was twelve. When this happened, *the Prince* moved out of state, and never had any further contact with his children. He never attended a graduation, wedding, or birth of his grandchildren, when Michelle was diagnosed with a brain tumor, he never showed up to support her, either before or after the surgery. Michelle and Maura went to New Mexico (where he moved) to try and reconnect and understand why he had abandoned them. He refused to even open the door. Proving what I had always stated

**Therapy expert accused of improper care**

**Therapist faces 'boundary' charge**

**Psychiatrist an expert witness on therapist's power over patient**

Corruption of Trust

– that his portrayal of "Father of the Year" was just that – a portrayal. His behavior and actions over the years have been devastating to his children. **The court system has no accountability for all their incorrect assumptions, predictions, and conclusions.**

Usually, women are too beaten down to follow through with complaints to the state boards about these injustices. It is the only thing available to them to try and mitigate the damage. **Labeling women as "crazy, bipolar, unstable, psychopathic, nuts, losers, greedy money grabbers", etc…is the cruelest form of intimidation and injustice.** Women are fighting for their children, yet this falls on deaf ears. It is a shocking fact that the court is deaf to a mother's desire not to lose her children. It is a form of intimidation that psychiatrists, psychologists, therapists, doctors, lawyers, and judges hold in their power because of their degrees and sense of entitled authority. This gives them unfair control, it shouldn't.

It is also a form of legal monetary extortion. It is also the legal trafficking of children, under the guise that it is in their best interests. Your entire future and that of your children is dependent on the sole discretion of an often compromised judge. Sometimes the system is too overwhelming for one person to change. If more people would just speak out either in the local arenas, or on social media, maybe this needed change would happen.

Often the agencies (local and federal) that are there to protect you are masters at not doing their job. More women need to take their complaints to the medical and regulatory boards. These archaic and unfair practices in family court need to be stopped. Women need to learn to use every setback and failure as steps to climb out of their despair from these unfair practices and leave the divorce/custody court system behind in the sewer, where it belongs.

On the other side, there are individuals like Marilyn VanDerbur, who spoke out, and started support groups on the effects of sexual abuse and incest on children at a young age. Forming a program called Survivors United Network (SUN). Before she had the courage to come forward, and bring this topic into the light, it was not spoken of or even recognized.

I am still fighting the City Government of Aspen – notorious for breaking the very laws they harshly enforce on certain citizens.

In the 1980s, some of the early residents joined forces against the ongoing assault on their way of life. We formed an organization called Private Sector Against Bureaucratic Sanctity (PSBS) and fought city hall. In 1987, we caught the city dumping street sweepings into the river. We watched as a city truck backed up to the Roaring Fork and dumped old coffee cups, dog waste, bubblegum wrappers, and all sorts of dirt and debris into the water. We confronted the city and, as usual, they denied any wrongdoing. Fortunately, we had taken pictures of their illegal activities. I went a step further. I gifted members of the city council some old fruit jars, filled with street sweepings of gum wrappers, cigarette butts, plastic, dog waste, and Styrofoam from the riverbanks. They had told us we needed to provide a "core sample" to prove our case that illegal dumping was polluting the river. They were not amused by my gift. The PSBS then wrote the Army Corps of Engineers with our evidence, and the city was fined by the Department of Health. We were vindicated. An editorial in the local newspaper carried the headline, "City loses Credibility When Its Employees Violate City Codes." For over a decade, the PSBS fought to remove the snowmaking machine, and the car impound lot off the Rio Grande property and helped develop this area into a park. Partly because of our campaign, it later was developed into John Denver Park, with waterfalls, walkways, and picnic benches. It went from an eyesore to a "Pride of Aspen" location.

During a minor remodel, they claimed that my front door was a hazard because it might become dangerous debris in the event of a flood. They tagged my sidewalk when I replaced the old, slick, unsafe redwood with cement. They red tagged every home improvement project or flood mitigation effort I made. I became a target. The city engineer came after me with anything he could dream up. I had a shed on the property line, and they ruled that it had to be moved back ten feet. I would have had to cut down large evergreens to relocate the shed. All the sheds in Aspen had always been on the property lines. It was ridiculous, and I fought it. The judge said I would be fined $300 a day if I didn't comply. I wasn't about to cut down trees to relocate a storage shed. Instead, I had the shed lifted onto a lowboy trailer and got it permitted as a camper, which brought it within the law.

Even recently, I was taken to court over my Kentucky Blue Grass. The city claimed I was growing invasive grass. It was easy to see it was not true just by looking at the fact that I had the same grass as everyone else who lived along the Roaring Fork River, and the same grass as the old art museum, John Denver Park, Newberry Park, and Herron Park, but the city made me hire my own attorney to prove it.

The Aspen Art Museum is, perhaps, the best example of

Denice and Keith - Aspen 2022

their hypocrisy. The 30,000 square foot structure was completed in 2014 over the objections of most of the residents, and in violation of the city's own building codes.

They violated all of their own laws to allow the museum to be built. Modern Aspen has become a place of rules and regulations, most which do not make sense, and are not applied evenly. Hypocrisy and corruption run rampant. I still have my home in Aspen, and I love it for what it once was, and represented. The story of what Aspen has become is a great disappointment. The pillage of Aspen, and the bullying tactics of its government need to change.

**I have changed, because a lot has changed for me. It took most of my life to teach people how I should be treated.** I learned to avoid arrogant people, who overwhelmed me with their "importance", learning their personalities were for display purposes only. They needed their insecurities and egos repaired regularly, and I was no longer available to them for that job. I no longer care about people's opinions of me, and do not let these opinions bother me. Remember, a wolf does not lose sleep over the opinions of the sheep he is about to eat. I learned to set limits on myself. I am no longer only a giver, and set limits because takers rarely do. I developed the confidence to let someone know that I loved them, but they are only a part of my history because they are no longer worth the pain and chaos they caused. It is not a great idea to keep a person around if they keep stabbing you, and pretend that they are the ones bleeding. **Never push a person to the point where they no longer care.**

In life, the best view comes from the highest climb out of despair. Strong people rarely have an easy past. **Being challenged is inevitable, but being defeated is optional.** Remember that doing the right thing when no one is watching is called integrity.

In life, most of the pieces are missing, and it is up to you to complete the puzzle over the years. **The last piece of the puzzle is often the best.** I have learned to surround myself with people who love and support me. There is no need to cut people off, when you grow, they will fall off eventually if they can not adapt to the changes. **In recent years, I have stopped waiting for my ship to come in. Instead, I swim out to meet it. I make my own happiness.**

My boldness paid off in spades when one day, at the encouragement of Michelle, I asked my dentist of forty years to have lunch with me, and he accepted. That lunch lasted three hours and we are now great companions. We have a wonderful romance. We go to the opera together and talk about everything. He treats me like I have always deserved to be treated. We share a deep respect for one another, and we laugh a lot. If I had hung onto the bitterness of my past, I would not have been able to embrace a relationship filled with laughter and joy. Keith is a lovely man and we agree that we went through most of our lives waiting for each other. Once again, I felt like I had won the lottery. **Being loved deeply gives you strength. Loving deeply gives you the courage to be yourself.** I am so lucky to have Michelle – a daughter and a friend, who always has my back – just as I have hers. I am also lucky to have Andrew. He has included me in his life, and makes me feel valued. He often thanks me for taking him to the classes at Home Depot, and his work ethic.

Another person I am lucky enough to have in my life is Kathy Brown. She is one of those friends who have stayed in my life the longest. We go every Saturday morning to our therapy sessions – the two of us garage and estate sale shopping, having coffee, and talking. For over forty years. Being with your best friend is all the therapy you need. I also have two great friends in Aspen, Cam and Leone – they still think I am a fun friend. I am very lucky.

Happiness does, indeed, come from within. In my case, it comes from challenging work and time with good friends and family.

With maturity, I have learned to accept the unacceptable, and use the betrayals, setbacks, and failures to create my success. Many people who are toxic have crossed my path in life, and I have learned the only way to win with them is not to play. I have also learned to no longer complain – it only defeats and destroys. **As Zig Ziglar said, if you are not willing to learn, no one can help you. If you are determined to learn, no one can stop you.**

The "experts" were the wrong people to share a shame story with. Their "understanding" and judgments of who you are, and their concentration on labeling you, their prescribing of dangerous medications, none of this is productive. It is not the "diagnosis" they give you; it is the strength and courage to get up and prove their predictions wrong that defines you, and your future. **When I joined SUN and the adoption group I could tell my story, and what I went through, it was so healing because it was someone else's story as well.**

Life has brought me many hardships, but also joy. I've learned that everything that happens can motivate us or destroy us. I choose motivation. Even though parts of my childhood were difficult, I learned from my time in Aspen and my parents. My father was my role model and my rock. My mother gave me the intense drive and defiant determination to be successful. I am also grateful to her for having the courage to take us to Aspen and for giving me my childhood of mineshafts, dumps, rivers, music, and the people and culture of the old wonderland of Aspen.

I was a broken little girl at times, who had to learn to get back up and not depend on others. **I am not what happened to me, I am what I chose to become.** Let children solve their own problems, and pick up their own toys, they need to feel their own worth. It helped create my future as a woman with strong, defiant determination. I enrolled in women's support groups, and their similar stories empowered me to understand my need for perfection, and my desire to avoid vulnerability. I learned to cherish the everyday, ordinary freedom of living. I took pride that I was not bitter. I took time to embrace every moment without the shame of the past that had motivated me for so long. I finally understood that I needed to forgive myself, and that my suicide attempt was merely a reaction and coping mechanism for the destruction of my spirit at such a young age. This enabled me to move out of the shame and into a new attitude. **I realized that the difficult people and times often teach us the most.** If you are not able to learn from these people and times, you get stuck and bitter, and stop living your life, instead living someone else's idea of your life.

I became stronger than I ever imagined and made better choices. I no longer tied my power to others expectations of me. I learned to take the last cookie on the plate as an act of self love that I was important, too. For over four decades, I was an energy machine, on the fast track to success. It was all I ever thought about. I wanted to be the best mother, the best realtor, I really only accepted failure in one area of my life - as a cook (my children always referred to my meals as, "burnt offerings"). There was never time for quiet reflection on this path to success. I was rarely finished with my day before 10pm.

I was a workaholic to protect myself from criticism and vulnerability. In all those years, I never stopped to think. I just ran toward achievement. When I lost everything in family court, I quit running. All those years brought me to the reality of, "So What?" That awful, difficult time was my teacher. It taught me to stop. It took a lot of courage to understand the setbacks and betrayals of my life, and humbled me into a quest of facing my demons.

**Women need to let go of the fairy tale.** We do not do ourselves or our daughters any favors by raising them to believe that a white knight will swoop in and give them a better life. We are not princesses. We are not delicate or fragile. **If we need to be saved, we need to learn to save ourselves.**

Every young woman should have the ability to live independently.

On the other side of my divorce, I found a contentment in liking what I now had, not what I did not have. I finally allowed myself to feel pride in my accomplishments. I realized that silence is often the best answer to stupid people. I am still learning not to respond to stupidity or arrogance – neither are repairable.

**Don't expect life to be fair – accept there is often no justice and move on.** Do not look back – you are not going that way. Choose to turn the negative pages, and don't read the book again. Recognize that there are people who get a great deal of joy out of "Tripping a Cripple," yet wear a cloak of innocence. Anger only keeps you bitter and depressed. It creates sorrow, and blinds you from seeing your own possibilities.

Broken people are not fragile, but often stronger in their broken places. It is as if time and experience mend these broken places together like glue. No matter how impressive someone's profession is, I have learned to question their conclusions....no longer naively trusting their judgements. It is a human system. People interject their own experiences, realities, and agendas.

**I have learned to use my voice to speak out, instead of letting people or systems silence me.** I learned trust is like a piece of fine china – once it is broken, it is worthless. When you're winning, keep competing like you're losing, and stay hungry. Learn how to fall, because you learn how to rise at the same time. I am no longer afraid to share my past – I want others to be empowered in life, and hope they are also able to climb out of their despair, realizing you only have your fingers to lift you up. I have always believed that good opportunities present themselves after difficult experiences. You don't drown by being pushed in the water; you drown by staying there. The bravest and best person you will ever meet is the person who still has an open heart after life's betrayals and setbacks. One day they may also tell the story of what they have overcome, and it will become part of someone else's survival guide. When people ask me what the biggest accomplishment was in my life, I reply - "The fact that I did not go insane."

As I have always said, "If it is meant to be, it is up to me." **Celebrate past victories, they empower you to go forward.** *We are the authors of our lives, and we write our own endings.*

I am now able to enjoy life. I like where I am. I know how it has turned out. I do not have to worry any longer about my career, or if my choice of a partner will make me happy, or who my children will become. I am no longer defined by other people or situations. I now have the gift of being able to look back on it all and acknowledge that I have always moved forward in a positive way and created a successful, satisfying, and meaningful life. A life that has been filled with love and laughter, despite all the setbacks.

If It Is Meant to Be, It Is up to Me

## Difficult People

Few things can make us feel crazier than expecting something from someone who nas nothing to give. Few things can frustrate us more than trying to make a person someone he or she isn't. we feel crazy when we try to pretend that person is someone he or she is not. We may have spent years negotiating with reallty concerning particular people from our past and our present. We may have spent years trying to get someone to loves us in a certain way, when that person cannot or will not.

It is time to let it go. It is time to let him or her go. That doesn't mean that we can't love that person anymore. It means that we will feel immense relief that comes when we stop denying reality and begin accepting. We release that person to be who he or she actually is.

We stop trying to make that person be someone he or she is not. We deal with our feelings and walk away from the destructive system.

We learn to love and care differently in a way that takes reality into account.

We enter into a relationsnp with that person on new terms—taking ourselves and our needs into account. If a perscr is addicted to atcohol, other drugs, misery, or other people, we let go of his or her acdiction; we take our hands off it. We give his or her life back. And we in the process, are given our life and freedom in return.

We stop letting what we are not getting from that person control us. We take responsibility for our life. WE go ahead with the process of loving and taking care of ourselves.

We decide how we want to interact with that person, taking reality and our own best interests into account. We get argry, we feel hurt, but we land in a pace of forgiveness. We set him or her free, and we become set free from bondage.

This is the heart of detaching in love.

December 4th daily meditation from Melody Beattie - I am printing with her permission, I read it daily

# Poems

Some poetry written throughout
my life which helped me heal.

—Denice

### Childhood Secrets
Deep within the soul
unmasked
Anguished hidden secrets of
the past
Imprisoned in a lifetime of
contrast
Those unspeakable acts
always last

### My Wedding Day
Fragile flower, unknowingly
Trusting harsh, bitter winds
To scatter me gently

## Marriage
There were the years of
sweet kisses
That let me pretend

There were four children
That healed the pain

There was always work
To validate my worth

There was an ever present
shadow
That kept me isolated and
Confused

There were many trophies
That hid the truth

There was the reality of
unspoken pain
That was painted in denial

There was a promise of life
beyond
that meant leaving his hard,
cruel bond

## The Batterer
I did not want to see his
Wrath
Confusing kisses and flowers
Today
Who is to say if I should
Walk away

## Adoption
Children come to weep,
Leaving their crumbs
Until no more joy to sweep.

## At Last 1995
No longer in the shadows of
his control
He screams in silence at his
shamed soul

My bitterness became
resistant
Immune to feel the cruel
contempt

Now, unafraid to hear what
others say
Outrageous courage
embraces me today

## Lawyers
Our Society must exist in
their reality
Not too sick, too angry, too
Successful, too anything
The more quiet, bland, and
Detached to life the more
The reward
We are a society of
Conformity with lawyers and
Judges
Often hiding the sickest of
Inner souls
Function well in the arena of
Power
Ever present in their
Detached façade

## Maturity
Accepting the Unacceptable
Today enduring calmness
Without a timetable

## To My Son
As the tender years disappear
There is no one left to hear
Silent memories still my
broken heart!

And so Andrew, my little dear
Careful not to shed a tear
Memories will cradle you
sweetheart!

In anguish I persevere,
Knowing the deception so clear
Someday there will be a heart
to heart!

The betrayal was mastered by
an engineer
The judge became the
auctioneer
And you and Mommy were
ordered to part!
Michelle declared their truth a
veneer
No one listened in this
Atmosphere

Shameless degradation broke
us apart!

Life can be so severe
Family, not what they appear

## Balloon
Winds of Terror
Swept us Alive
Crashing in Breathless
Despair
Elated my children
Survive

## Future
As I learn to paddle alone
all I valued to stone

Now ..A lonely survivor
Free to find a new river

Gliding down the middle ever
more
Careful not to attach to a shore

Floating by all life's bait
Nothing more to advocate

Only water boards my boat
And is easily thrown out

## Growth
So much love within
Rediscovering the self
Through all the hidden pain

## The Journey
Sometimes at a young age, we
learn to hang on tightly
To a life raft, overloaded
with expectations, myths,
And attachments to
outcome.

After years of holding on…
in the tossing
Waves of life's lessons, we
begin to let go of that
Destructive chaos.
We stop negotiating reality
and release the raft…in
order
To swim unburdened. There
we find the end is
Actually in the calmness of
Our New Beginning

Made in the USA
Las Vegas, NV
14 November 2022